167 Tax Tips for Canadian Small Business 2009

beat the taxman to keep more money in your business

Updated for the 2008 tax year

STEPHEN THOMPSON, CA, CFP, TEP

John Wiley & Sons Canada, Ltd.

John Wiley & Sons Canada, Ltd.
6045 Freemont Blvd., Mississauga, Ontario, L5R 4J3

Library and Archives Canada has catalogued this publication as follows:

Thompson, Stephen (Stephen Douglas)
  167 Tax tips for Canadian small business 2009: beat the taxman to keep more money in your business / Stephen Thompson.

Annual.
[1997]-
Includes index.
ISSN 1707-3553
ISBN-13: 978-0-470-15974-3 (2009 edition for the 2008 tax year)

1997-2008 eds. published under title:
Beat the taxman!: easy ways to save tax in your small business

1. Small business—Taxation—Law and legislation—Canada—Popular works. 2. Tax planning—Canada—Popular works. 3. Home-based businesses—Taxation—Canada—Popular works. I. Title.

HJ4662.A3T46   343.7106   C2003-300958-9

Production Credits
Cover Design: Ian Koo
Inteior design: Natalia Burobina
Printer: Tri-Graphic Printing Ltd.
Printed and bound in Canada

1 2 3 4 5 TRI 13 12 11 10 09

Contents

Year-Round
Tax-Planning Calendar

January

- Don't forget to record your odometer reading on the 1st for allowable automobile deductions. (Page 167)

- Pay interest on funds borrowed from your spouse or parent used for investing to avoid attribution by the 30th. (Page 41-42)

February

- Have you paid a family member EI? If so, consider applying for a ruling to make them EI exempt. (Page 49)

- Deadline for filing T4 Short, T4, T4A, and T4F Summary and Supplementary is the 28th. (Page 120)

March

- Deadline for making your 2008 RRSP contribution is the 1st (unless extended by the government).

- First 2009 tax instalment due on the 15th. (Page 110)

April

- Review flexible deductions such as RRSP contributions, CCA, and allowance for doubtful accounts to ensure you maximize your tax rate stairway. (Pages 52, 56, 57)

- Deadline for filing personal income tax returns is the 30th unless you or your spouse carry on an unincorporated business. If you owe tax, the liability is still due on April 30th. (Page 107)

- The 30th is the last day in which to file a Notice of Objection for your 2007 tax return if you or your spouse did not carry on an unincorporated business in 2007. (Page 199)

May

- Consider hiring your children in your business over the summer and save. (Page 43)

June

- Deadline for filing personal income tax returns if you or your spouse carry on an unincorporated business is the 15th. (Page 107)

- Second 2009 tax instalment due on the 15th. (Page 110)

- The 15th is the last day in which to file a Notice of Objection for your 2007 tax return if you or your spouse carried on an unincorporated business in 2007. (Page 199)

- The 15th is the deadline for filing the GST annual return for unincorporated businesses with a December year-end and that file on an annual basis. (Page 97)

July

- Review your instalment options for the upcoming tax instalment. (Page 111)

August

- Review your tax assessment notice to ensure it agrees with how you filed your tax return. Investigate any significant differences. (Page 195)

- If you have been charged penalties or interest, consider if you can get them reversed. (Page 205)

September

- Third 2009 tax instalment due on the 15th. (Page 110)

October

- If you're considering using the Quick Method for the GST, apply now for the upcoming year. (Page 85)

November

- Review your instalment options for the upcoming final 2009 tax instalment. (Page 111)

December

- Fourth 2009 tax instalment due on the 15th. (Page 110)

- First and only tax instalment is due on the 31st for farmers and fisherman. (Page 110)

- Value your inventory and consider writing off obsolete or damaged inventory if you have a December year-end. (Page 136)

- Consider purchasing now, any major asset you're planning to buy early next year if you have a December year-end. (Page 155)

- Consider delaying until next year the sale of any major asset if you have a December year-end. (Page 156)

- If you have a December year-end and can use the cash method of accounting, consider deferring tax by purchasing some of next year's supplies this month. (Page 22)

- Record your odometer reading for calculating allowable automobile deductions by the end of the month. (Page 167)

Preface

Beat the Taxman! had its beginnings about seventeen years ago in the form of a "Lunch and Learn" seminar that we created for our clients. The seminars focused on easy tax-planning ideas for the individual investor and businessperson. Several of the ideas discussed in this book originated in those seminars. The main philosophy of the seminars also became the main philosophy of this book: That saving tax dollars involves doing a lot of little things right, throughout the year.

While it's true that under the right circumstances significant tax dollars can be saved using complex structures and high-level tax plans, it is also important to realize that really effective tax planning starts with knowing the rules and doing a lot of little things correctly throughout the year. Tax planning doesn't occur on April 30 when you file your tax return. It occurs when you're planning to purchase that new vehicle, when you're paying your teenage son or daughter that monthly allowance, and when you're recording the revenue and expenses of the business. Tax planning is truly a 365-day-a-year fight. And this book is meant to help you win that fight.

In this book, tax savings is definitely the name of the game. My focus from the outset has been on how I can save you tax dollars. In order to accomplish this task, I have had to explain some of the tax legislation so that I can show you how to use it to your advantage. However, I have intentionally kept the tax explanations short, to the point, and not too complex. My objective is to save you tax, not teach you tax law.

I have also structured the book in an easy-to-understand question-and-answer format. This will allow you to quickly go to a section that relates to your business. For the most part, the chapters of the book, or what I refer to as "Rounds," stand alone. That is to say, you do not have to read the book from start to finish in the order that I have laid out. If a section does not relate to your business, you can skip that section and move on. Where the rules interrelate I refer you to the sections where they are explained in more detail.

I do, however, recommend at least a cursory review of the sections of the book which you believe do not relate to your business. My experience has been that many taxpayers believe certain legislation does not apply to them until they obtain more information. You can save taxes by knowing the rules and acting on them.

TAX BEATER

Deduct the cost of this book and save.

Throughout the book I have highlighted important tax-planning ideas by summarizing them in the margins as "Tax Beaters." In the body of the text that runs beside the Tax Beaters, I have explained in more detail how to use the technique to save tax dollars. For example, if you are in business or you are in receipt of commission income, you can deduct the cost of this book as a business expense. If you are in the highest personal income tax level of about 50%, this idea will save you approximately $13.50. As well, if your business is registered for GST, you will be eligible for an input tax credit of approximately $1.35 on the purchase of this book. This is a savings of approximately $14.85 depending on your province and tax level. In this way I have tried to make tax savings easy and time effective.

For quick reference I have placed at the end of the book a summary of all 167 Tax Beaters plus three bonus tax tips.

Some Words of Caution

It is impossible to predict every potential tax situation and include it in this book. And, as I mentioned earlier, my focus is on tax savings, not on tax education. I have made a concerted effort to provide an accurate summary of what I consider to be the more important areas in the tax law that was in effect at the time of writing this book, and as that law relates to small and home-based businesses. Many of the ideas in this book are very straightforward. However, there are several areas that are more complex and for which you may need assistance. You should always consider seeking the advice of an expert to ensure that a tax saving idea is right for you. This book is not intended to be a substitute for good professional tax advice.

It is also important to realize that what may make perfectly good sense from an income tax savings point-of-view, may make little sense when reviewed in your particular business situation. I have concentrated on ways to use the income tax legislation to your advantage. However, it is important for you to decide if the ideas make sense in your business. This is a personal assessment which only you and your tax advisor can make.

Acknowledgements

I would like to thank Popi Xanthos, CA, for her assistance in updating this year's edition of *Beat the Taxman!* Popi is a senior CA in our office and a graduate of the CICA In-Depth tax course. Popi's efforts were instrumental in ensuring that this year's edition happened. I want to thank her for her contributions.

Get Off to
a Good Start

$\mathbf{A}$s with many things in life, starting off right in business can often make the difference between winning the match or getting knocked out before the first bell. Knowing where you stand with the Canada Revenue Agency (formerly Revenue Canada) and what the ground rules are going to be can pay dividends to you down the road. In this round, we will look at some of the key questions that are often asked when starting up a new business and how to turn these questions into tax-saving ideas.

What Is a Business?

What is a business? This seems like a pretty straightforward question, one hardly worth spending any time on at all. But, in fact, it is absolutely the first question to ask when you're starting up, and essential for getting started on the right foot.

You may find this statement surprising, but I have found that the Canada Revenue Agency and the typical Canadian taxpayer do not always agree! A key area of disagreement concerns the question "What is a business?" In fact, the Canada Revenue Agency (CRA), the courts and taxpayers have been

arguing a lot about what is and what is not a business over the
past few decades. What would seem to be a straightforward
question has been a very difficult fundamental question to answer. And the problem has historically come about because
CRA does not want to allow a taxpayer to deduct losses year
over year in a questionable business. As a result, in the past,
the tax department considered a business to be any activity
that you conduct for a profit or a reasonable expectation of
a profit. If the business could not demonstrate that it could
become profitable, CRA would deny the losses.

On May 23, 2002, the Supreme Court of Canada ruled
on two cases, Stewart v. The Queen and the Queen v. Walls,
which changed all the rules. As a result of the Supreme Court
of Canada's decision, CRA now only considers the concept of
"reasonable expectation of profit" if there is a personal element with respect to your business. If there is no personal or
hobby element and assuming of course your business is not a
sham, then CRA will generally no longer question whether or
not you are in fact in business.

If, however, there is a personal or hobby element in your
business, then it must be determined if your business is carried on in a sufficiently commercial manner as to indicate that
there would be a source of income, and therefore a business.
In this case, CRA would look at whether or not there is a reasonable expectation of profit from your enterprise so that it
may be considered a legitimate business.

It would appear, however, that the federal government
was not entirely happy with the Supreme Court of Canada's
decision in the Stewart and Walls cases, for on October 31,
2003 the Department of Finance released proposed amendments that would essentially reverse the court's decision
and legislate the former CRA's assessing practices. That is,
to deny business losses and other expenses unless there is a
reasonable expectation of profit from that business or related activity. Originally, it was intended that if this proposed
new section of the Income Tax Act became law, it would
be effective for taxation years starting after 2004. What the

Department of Finance found was that during the period of public consultation, many individuals and groups expressed serious concerns that a test to determine whether a reasonable expectation of profit exists may unintentionally limit a number of ordinary commercial expenses. As a result, the Department has decided to revise the legislation in order to address the concerns of the public while still achieving the Government's objectives. In the fall of 2005, the Department of Finance stated that its intention was to replace the concept of "reasonable expectation of profit" with a more modest concept, however, at the time of writing no further details had been provided. Since 2005, there has been no mention of this issue in any federal budget. So, for now, we must wait until the Department of Finance issues its alternate proposal for the public to comment on. Until new legislation actually comes into force, the Canada Revenue Agency has publicly announced that they are assessing based on the Stewart and Walls cases. Therefore, for now, it is best to understand CRA's current assessing practice.

Based on the Supreme Court of Canada's decision there is now a two-step process in deciding what is and what is not a business for tax purposes. If your business has no personal element involved, then it will normally be considered a business. If the business is not successful, the Canada Revenue Agency will normally allow the losses. In the very recent past, CRA would try to deny legitimate business losses on the premise that there was no reasonable expectation of profit, therefore no source of income or no business. Now, under their current assessing practises, if there is no personal or hobby element, CRA will generally have to allow the losses. This is a major win for the taxpayer as many legitimate businesses have lost over the years their right to claim losses from what amounted to bad business decisions.

However, if there is a personal or hobby element to your business then you have to move to step two in the process. In this step, it must be determined if your business is being carried on in a sufficiently commercial manner as to still qualify as a source of income and thereby qualify as a business. To determine whether or not your business is carried on sufficiently in a commercial manner, CRA will use among other tools, the concept of reasonable expectation of profit. But the anticipation of profit cannot be the only test used by CRA. The objective is to evaluate the commercial nature of your activity, not to judge your business acumen. Therefore, even though your business may not be profitable and there is a personal element involved, losses from the business can still be tax deductible if your business is operated in a sufficiently commercial nature.

Developing examples of how these rules would work is tricky, as CRA is just starting to announce how they plan to interpret the new rules. However, it is probably safe to go through some extreme examples to highlight how these concepts are likely to be interpreted. First of all, if your business is profitable, then you likely have very little to worry about. CRA is mostly concerned with taxpayers deducting business losses. Profitable businesses will normally be considered in business provided that your activity is not on account of capital. Income on account of capital is normally a single transaction that results in a gain. Instead, we are assuming your business has many transactions and therefore the income would be considered business income.

Now let's say you have a ceramics business and the ceramics you make are for a local electronics manufacturer. The ceramics have no value, other than to your customer, as it is a component in the product they are making. You do no other types of ceramics. Despite your best efforts however you have not been able to turn a profit. It is hard to suggest that there would be any personal element in this business. Accordingly, we do not have to look at whether or not you will ever be profitable. You are operating a commercial activity and your business losses would be tax deductible.

Now let's say you only make cute ceramic statues. You would like to sell them to the public but after three years you have only been successful in selling a couple to strangers and a few to family members. You on the other hand have a nice collection of the statues in your home. In this case you are most likely operating a hobby or at least there is a definite personal element to your business. So the question becomes have you been operating it in a sufficiently commercial nature as to suggest that your losses should be deductible as a business loss. To determine this you might look at your business plan, whether anything happened unexpectedly that caused your business to become unsuccessful and what effort did you make to correct the matter. If however, your business is really just a hobby, then your losses will not be tax deductible. Not so much because it was not profitable, but because you really never engaged the business in a sufficiently commercial manner.

The above represents the current assessing practices of CRA. However, as mentioned earlier, the government was proposing some changes to the legislation that many thought would dramatically affect the deductibility of losses and expenses in the future. The legislation that was being proposed would have only allowed the deduction of business losses and other expenses where it would have been reasonable to assume that you would realize a cumulative profit from the business during the time that you carried on the business or could reasonably be expected to have carried on the business. The concept of whether or not there is a personal element to your business would be gone. If you could expect to realize a cumulative profit, then you would be able to deduct the losses. If you did not, or could not, realize a cumulative profit then the losses would have been denied. For clarity, profit would not have included capital gains from the selling of the business or asset. So if you were intending on operating a business at a loss with the intention of selling the underlying assets for a gain a few years later, then your losses would likely not have been deductible because there would not have been a cumulative profit, given that the gain on the sale would not be considered as a part of the profit.

It is important to note that this test for reasonable expectation of profit would have been an annual test, one that if questioned you would have to defend to the Canada Revenue Agency. As an example, it is possible that the first few years of operation you managed your business at a loss but that it is sensible to consider that your business has a reasonable expectation of making a cumulative profit. However, say in year four, it is no longer reasonable to expect that the business can operate with a cumulative profit. Accordingly, in year four and subsequent years your losses would be denied. It becomes apparent from this that it would have been increasingly important to document exceptional events that prevented you from being profitable and to prepare and revise your business plan to support your reasonable expectation of profit.

Again, the important thing to remember is that this is how the legislation would have operated had it been passed. As was mentioned earlier, the Federal government is currently revising its proposed legislation in order to address the concerns that were raised. Until their revised legislation is made public, we won't know what the new rules will entail and how much of a compromise the government will make. However, by having an understanding of what the original legislation looked like we gain an idea of where the government is going.

As you can see, determining whether or not your business is in fact a business for tax purposes can be a difficult question to answer. The changes in the rules and interpretations continue to complicate an already difficult and sensitive area. In the end, if you truly believe your business is legitimate but is merely struggling, claim the losses and document as best you can the reasons why your business will be successful. If you are ever challenged by Canada Revenue Agency, seek a good tax coach and argue your position. This is a fight you will want to win.

Should I Keep My Losses Low in the Start-Up Years?

Sometimes legitimate business operators fear that if they claim too great a loss or if they have too many years in a row with losses, that the Canada Revenue Agency will disallow the deduction of the loss. Some even fail to deduct expenses to reduce the loss or, even worse, generate income and pay tax on it to show an expectation of profit. This type of "tax planning" is totally unwarranted. If you are operating a legitimate business, always deduct all legitimate business expenses to reduce your tax liability. If challenged, with a good tax coach in your corner, you can often successfully argue your case and, by obtaining a favourable ruling, "Beat the Taxman."

TAX BEATER
Report all legitimate business expenses even if you incur persistent losses.

If your business is continuing to incur losses, instead of not deducting legitimate expenses, look at your business to see what expenses can be reduced or eliminated that would make your business profitable. Can you, for example, pay down debt which will reduce your interest expense or reduce some office or other business expenses.

If your business has a personal element involved and is not profitable, then you may need to show that it has a reasonable expectation of profit or that it is being carried on in a sufficiently commercial manner. Often the best support to turn too for this is your business plan. I strongly recommend that you prepare a business plan complete with forecasts of revenues and expenses for your business regardless whether there is a personal element involved or not. The business plan will serve as the documentary proof that your business can be successful and that you embarked with full intentions of making a profit. If later your business is unsuccessful, you will have something to compare too to see what happened. If you can identify one or more "events" that happened or didn't happen that resulted in losses to your business, then these "events" can be used to show to a tax official that at the time of starting the business there was a reasonable expectation of profit if not for these "events," and that the losses should be deductible.

When Did My Business Start?

In order to maximize your tax savings when starting a business, it is important to know when your business began. For example, did your business start when you made your first

TAX BEATER
Record all business-related expenses between startup and your first sale.

sale, or met with your first customer? Or did your business begin when you opened your new bank account, installed the separate telephone line, or purchased your first supplies?

It can often be months after this start-up date before sales finally start happening. If you consider your business to have started only after your first sale, then you may lose out on some significant tax deductions.

There are no hard and fast rules on when a business starts. The beginning date is very much dependent on the facts of each particular case. Generally speaking, a business is considered to commence whenever some significant activity is started which is important for the operation of the business. For example, a business may be considered to have started when you begin applying for a licence necessary to operate your business, or when you make your first purchase of supplies or products to sell.

Any expenses made before the start of a business will not be tax deductible. So before you incur significant costs relating to your business, perform some event which will signify the beginning of your operation. This event may be the registering of your business name with the province or the Chamber of Commerce, or opening up a separate bank account. Whatever it is, do something that signifies the start of operations.

| **TAX BEATER** |
| Don't spend money on your business before official startup. |

What Types of Expenses Can I Deduct?

Generally speaking, any reasonable expense that relates to your business is tax deductible. From this basic rule, there are numerous restrictions which the government has legislated to reduce the tax deductions. These restrictions are discussed throughout the book. By knowing these restrictions you can plan around them and maximize your tax deductions.

| **TAX BEATER** |
| The general rule: All reasonable business-related expenses are tax deductible. |

Am I Really Self-Employed or Still an Employee?

This is an important distinction. If you think you are self-employed but the Canada Revenue Agency later decides you are still an employee, then many of the expenses you have tried to deduct may be denied. Additionally, your employer will be required to pay Canada Pension Plan contributions and Employment Insurance and may be assessed interest and penalties for not remitting these payments along with the withholding tax on your "salary."

In many cases it is obvious that you are self-employed: you have several different customers, you are your own boss, you supply your own tools, and you have the risk of losing money. However, there are many cases where this distinction is much more blurred. In today's world of downsizing, many employers are laying off their staff and hiring contract workers. Often, an employee is given a retirement package and then asked to come back on a contract basis. If this has happened to you, are you an employee or self-employed?

The distinction between being an employee and being self-employed is based on the facts of each case. Over the years the courts have developed four tests that they use to determine if you are an employee or self-employed. These tests are:

1. The control test
2. The integration or organization test
3. The economic reality test
4. The specific results test

The Control Test: If one person holds considerable control over you, in the form of deciding what you will do, how you do it, when you do it, and where you do it, then they may be considered to be your employer. If, on the other hand, you have the liberty to perform the task as you choose, provided it is done within an agreed-upon time, then you may pass this test.

TAX BEATER
Know and follow the rules for self-employment.

The Integration or Organization Test: This test looks at whether or not you become an integral part of an organization. If your work is so closely tied to your customer's business that you act like any other employee, then you may also be considered to be an employee.

The Economic Reality Test: This is often the most clear-cut test. It looks at whether or not you own your own tools, have a chance to make a profit, or could be at risk of incurring a loss. Where an individual supplies no funds or tools, takes no financial risks and has no liability, the courts have considered the relationship to be employee and employer.

The Specific Results Test: This last test looks at whether or not you are performing a specific task with a distinct completion or whether your services are provided over an extended time frame, with no specific result contemplated. An employee is typically hired to perform various tasks as required on an ongoing basis. A self-employed person would be hired to perform a specific task, the completion of which would end the relationship.

As you can see, these rules are complex and you may wish to seek the assistance of a professional. However, by knowing these rules you may be able to arrange your affairs in such a way that supports your treatment as a self-employed individual. Being self-employed will allow you to deduct all legitimate business expenses from the start-up date of your business and will help you win Round 1.

Keep accurate Records— and Save!

The most often overlooked opportunity to save taxes is keeping adequate business records. I have seen many taxpayers pay excessive taxes simply because they did not create a system that allowed them to keep track of and record all of their business expenses. This round will look at how an effective record-keeping system will help you "Beat the Taxman."

Why Should I Take the Time to Keep Records?

You can save taxes. (Doesn't that make the tedium worth it?)

Most small-business entrepreneurs don't like to spend the time to record their business transactions. It distracts them from what they believe really makes them money, their business. However, I believe that an effective record-keeping system can also make you money, by saving you tax dollars. Good records help to ensure that you are reporting all expenses that relate to your business. This will save tax dollars when you do your tax return.

TAX BEATER

Record all expenses to save tax dollars.

Record-keeping doesn't have to take a lot of your time; the key to an effective record-keeping system is to keep it simple. Whether you use a computer or record your transactions manually, you want the process to be quick and easy. You want a system where you can record all revenue and expenses, but you don't have to spend most of the day doing bookkeeping. When your business becomes more complicated, your record-keeping system can become more complex. But until then, keep it simple.

You can avoid hassles with Canada Revenue Agency. (Definitely worth it!)

Another reason for keeping records is that the government says you must. This works for them, but it also works for you.

By keeping accurate records you can protect yourself. In criminal law, you're considered innocent until proven guilty. If you've done something wrong, the authorities must prove it. However, with tax law, if there is a dispute, you're normally considered guilty until you can prove your innocence.

TAX BEATER

Accurate records can help you prove your case to Canada Revenue Agency.

The reason for this "reverse judgement" is that the income tax system is self-assessing. You tell the government what your income is and they, for the most part, accept this declaration. If they decide to check your return and challenge you on any of your deductions, it is up to you to prove to them that all of your revenue is recorded and that all of your expenses are legitimate. The best way to prove this is to produce the records of your business, complete with bank statements and original invoices.

If you cannot produce any records for the Canada Revenue Agency, they are less likely to accept the figures that you have reported on your tax return. Should this occur, you will end up paying considerably more taxes than you originally expected. Therefore, keeping proper records can save you hassles in the long run and, more importantly, can save you tax dollars.

In addition, good records can help to ensure that you are claiming all legitimate expenses. More deductions means less tax and you winning Round 2 with the Taxman.

For How Long Do I Have to Keep My Records?

If you file your income tax returns on time, you must keep your records for a minimum of six years after the end of the year to which they relate. For example, you must keep the records for your 2002 taxation year until the end of the year 2008. You can reduce this six-year requirement if you cease your business operations.

If you file your tax return late, then you must keep your records for six years after the date you filed that tax return. For example, if you filed your 2001 tax return in 2003, then you must keep your records until the end of the year 2009.

If you wish to destroy your records before the minimum time frame is up, then you must get permission from Canada Revenue Agency. To obtain this permission, you can complete form T137 "Request for Destruction of Books and Records" and forward it to your local district taxation office. Alternatively, you can write to the director of your local district taxation office requesting permission to destroy records. This letter must be signed by an authorized representative of your business and should contain the following information:

1. a clear identification of books, records, or other documents to be destroyed;
2. the taxation year for which the request applies;
3. details of any special circumstances which would justify destruction of the books and records at an earlier time than that normally permitted; and
4. any other pertinent information.

What Information Should I Keep?

There are no rules that say precisely what type of records you need to keep. In most cases, the complexity of the business will dictate the complexity of the records. However, as a minimum you should keep the following:

- all original source documents, like invoices and receipts for your expenses
- bank statements, cancelled cheques, and your copy of the bank deposit slip
- your copy of your own invoices and receipts

And, in most cases, you must keep a summary of the year's transactions. This summary could be a simple listing of the various revenue and expense amounts, or it can be a more detailed computerized general ledger produced by one of the many accounting software packages available on the market.

If you have electronic records (e.g., if you use a commercial accounting software package), you must keep your records in an electronically readable and accessible format even if you have paper copies of the data. Also, if any of your electronic records are lost, destroyed or damaged, you are required to report this situation to your local tax services office, and you must recreate the files within a reasonable period of time. In order to ensure that you don't accidentally lose or delete any electronic business data, you should always make sure that this information has been backed-up to either a computer hard drive, CD, floppy disk or some other type of re-writable media.

TAX BEATER
Make sure that you have an up-to-date back up of any electronic records.

What If I Don't Get a Receipt?

One of the most common reasons why small-business entrepreneurs pay more than their fair share of taxes is because they forget to record all of their expenses. It is easy to forget those expenses when you don't get a receipt.

Even in the cases where you don't get a receipt, you can still deduct the expense. Write in your records the details of the transaction, such as the item purchased, the name and address of the supplier, the date of the transaction, and the amount you paid. This should allow you to get the tax deduction for the expense.

TAX BEATER
Even without a receipt you can still claim an expense.

However, whenever possible, try to get a receipt from your supplier. This will help you remember to record the transaction and provide proof of the expense.

What If There Is No Description on a Receipt?

In order for an expense to be deductible, it must be reasonable and it must relate to your business. If your receipts do not indicate what the payment was for, there is no way for you to prove that the expense was for your business.

In most cases, suppliers will provide a description on their invoices. However, sometimes you may receive a cash register receipt that has no description. In this case, write on the receipt a quick description of the purchase. By doing so, you will still be able to deduct the expense in the business.

> **TAX BEATER**
> Where no description shows on a receipt, itemize the purchase yourself.

How Can I Develop a Simple Record-Keeping System?

Method A: To each its own ... envelope

Recording the transactions for your small business does not have to be complicated. The simplest method for keeping track of your business expenses is to create a separate envelope for each expense and revenue category. For example, if your business is a song-writing and recording studio, expense categories could include "office supplies," "computer and accessories," "advertising," and revenue categories could include "studio rental," "song-writing," and "radio jingle production."

As you incur the expense or receive the revenue, place each receipt in its envelope. At the end of the year, total each envelope and enter the information on your tax return.

This system is very simple and for very small businesses it can be quite adequate. However, if your business is somewhat more complex, this system may not be sufficient to keep track of all of your expenses. This may result in you missing deductions and losing the round with the taxman.

Method B: For wanna-be bookkeepers

A more complicated, yet still relatively simple, system is to combine the method above, of keeping a separate envelope for each expense and revenue category, with recording the transactions. To record your transactions, all you need is some columnar paper. You can buy pads of 14-column paper that are pre-ruled for easy financial record-keeping.

Along the top of the columns list your major revenue and expense categories. Then, at the end of each week, record each revenue or expense transaction in the proper column. By recording the transactions weekly you are more likely to record all expenses. If you leave the recording of the transactions to the end of the month, you're more likely to forget to record your small purchases.

The advantage with this system is that it is simple and, in cases where there are few transactions, it can be very effective. However, where there are many transactions this system can perform miserably. The main problem is that there is no balancing of the transactions, so you can't check your addition or check your record against your bank account to ensure that all transactions have been recorded. If you have more than 150 transactions a year, consider moving to the next level of record-keeping.

Method C: "Doing the double-entry"

The next level of record-keeping is referred to as the "double-entry" system. With this system you record your transactions in such a way that you can easily tell if you have made an addition error or placed an item in the wrong column. When you are trying to record hundreds of transactions during the year, a misplaced expense in a revenue column can mean hundreds or even thousands of dollars in additional taxes paid to the government. This system prevents such accidents, reduces taxes, and keeps you fighting the Taxman.

With double-entry record-keeping, you should still use envelopes or file folders to keep all of your receipts by major

TAX BEATER
Record your transactions weekly so you don't forget a business expense.

TAX BEATER
Use a double-entry record-keeping system to avoid costly mistakes.

revenue and expense category. Use columnar paper as before, to list each major revenue and expense category across the top of the columns. However, this time, reserve the first three numeric columns for bank deposits, bank withdrawals, and your personal account. Then list your expense and revenue categories. Finally, reserve the last column for miscellaneous expenses.

Now, under the title of each of the columns, write a positive or a negative sign. Bank deposits are a positive, bank withdrawals are a negative. Because your personal account could be either, place a positive and a negative sign. Sales are a negative and all of the expense accounts are a positive. Now you're ready to start recording transactions.

Every transaction you record should equal zero when added across the page. For example, if you were to record a sale of $100, you would enter $100 in the bank deposit column and $100 in the sale column. The bank deposit column is a positive $100 and the sale column is a negative $100; when added together they equal $0.

Here's another example. Say you paid $50 for some business supplies on your personal credit card account, you would enter $50 as a negative in the personal account and $50 under the supplies (expense) account. When these two are added together they equal zero.

Date	Description	Bank		Personal	Sales	Supplies	Auto
		Deposits +	Withdrawals −	+/−	−	+	+
Feb 5	Sale—Mr. Brown	100 —			100 —		
Feb 5	ABC Stationary			<50 —>		50 —	

If you are unsure about an entry, try a little trick I use. Always start with the side of the entry you're sure about. With the personal credit card entry, you know you want to add $50 to the supplies account, so enter it on the record. Now you need a negative to get the line to balance and you know the money did not come from the business bank account, it came from your personal account. So the negative must go in the personal account column as a negative.

The double-entry record-keeping system is much more effective in keeping track of all of your business expenses. It is less likely that addition errors will go unnoticed and much more likely that all expenses will be recorded. This process can also be placed on the computer using a simple spreadsheet.

Method D: The Computerized Approach

The last alternative is to perform your record-keeping using an off-the-shelf or customized computer software. There are many software packages on the market and most, if not all, are excellent programs. The real trick with computerizing your record-keeping is to find a software package that meets your business needs and your computer and bookkeeping abilities. Here are some things to consider when deciding on an accounting software program:

- Ensure that the software you are looking at is in fact an accounting software program and not a personal finance program. Personal finance programs are excellent for looking after your personal revenues and expenses and establishing net worth amounts and other functions. However, when it comes to recording the transactions for your business, these programs are generally not up to the job. That is not the task for which they were designed.

  Under Method B, I mentioned that a major shortfall of just recording transactions is that there is no balancing and checking to ensure that you have not entered or added an amount incorrectly. This can be a problem with personal financial programs. Some of these programs allow you to enter one sided entries and make other bookkeeping errors without warning you that a potential error has occurred.

So, I would recommend that you stick with an accounting software package designed for business use if you wish to computerize your record-keeping. You will be thankful in the long-run.

- When looking at accounting software, you should keep in mind the complexity of your business. If your operations are very straightforward, and are likely to stay that way, then you are going to want a software package that is easy to use and performs the basic functions you need. However, if your business activity and structure is very complex, then a more advanced package may be for you. Determining factors generally include, but are not limited to, the ability of the program to deal with a large number of customers, vendors, or inventory items, more than one business operation or division and how it can tie these operations together, the ability to network multiple users, and the ability to deal with foreign currency transactions.

- Look at the comprehensiveness of the software and whether or not there are additional modules that can be purchased later in case your business expands. Some programs are very comprehensive and have all of the functions you could ever want. And, if you need them right now, then maybe this is the program for you. On the other hand, some programs give you the basics that you need and then you can purchase additional modules later as your business becomes more complex. This ability to expand is important since you are not going to want to learn a new software program once you have invested time and energy in one program. So make sure the software can expand to meet your needs as your business grows.

- Review the recommended system requirements for optimum use of the software. The accounting software package will usually clearly state what your minimum computer requirements should be in order for the program to run effectively. If you have less than the minimum, you may need to upgrade your hardware, which may make the software purchase very expensive.

- Your bookkeeping skills and accounting knowledge are also important factors to keep in mind. Some programs take very little accounting skill and very little set-up. If you know how to write a cheque and fill in the cheque register, then you can record transactions in the software. Other programs take hours of set-up and require more accounting skill. There are benefits and disadvantages to both. Consider your skills when selecting a program. It will reduce your frustrations considerably.

- If you use an accounting firm to help with the preparation of your financial statements and tax returns, talk to them to see if there is a program that they use or prefer. Since you will be working closely with your accounting firm, purchasing a software they use regularly will make it easy for them to advise you on set-up, posting year-end adjustments, and ongoing maintenance of your records.

- Enquire as to support for the program. There are two types of support. Technical support for the operation of the program and accounting support for the setting up and recording of transactions. Most manufacturers will supply you with technical support. However you may have to look elsewhere for support on how to use the software, record transactions, and maximize the use of the software. Places to look to learn about the software include your accountant, private training facilities, your software supplier, and community colleges.

- The last item you should always keep in mind is the cost of the program. Unfortunately, this often becomes the only consideration. But how good is an inexpensive piece of software to you if it doesn't do what you need and you can't get anyone to show you how to use it. Cost is important and should always be kept in mind. But it should not be the only determining factor.

Using computer software to record the business activity will require more work on your part and often more frustrations. However, if your business has many transactions, the computer is often the only way to go.

How Do I Know If I Made Money?

So you've been diligent and have been recording all of your transactions throughout the year. Now you want to know if you made any money! An easy way to see how much money you made is to complete the income schedule provided in the Appendix, which is set up under the same format as the information requested by the Canada Revenue Agency on their form T2124, "Statement of Business Activities." This government form is used by sole proprietors or partners to report their business income on their personal tax returns.

From your records, add up all of your revenue columns and insert them on the income line. If you have inventory, enter your opening inventory amount, add to that the amount of your purchases. Now subtract your closing inventory. This will provide you with a cost of goods sold figure. Next insert all of your expenses. If you have capital assets, calculate the proper depreciation amount as discussed in Round 9.

Finally, subtract from revenue the cost of goods sold, your expenses, and the depreciation. You can perform this exercise every month using this format to see how your business is doing.

Can I Use the Cash Method for Reporting Business Income?

In most cases, you will not be able to use the cash method for reporting business income. The exceptions are if you are a self-employed commission sales agent or a fisherman or farmer. In all other cases you will have to use the accrual method for reporting business income.

What Is the Cash Accounting Method?

The cash accounting method for reporting business income allows a limited number of taxpayers to report income in the year they receive it and deduct expenses in the year they pay them. For example, if you sold a product but have not received the cash, you don't have to report the income. Once you receive the cash, then you report the sale. With this method you only include in income cash received during the year and you only record as an expense purchases paid during the year.

TAX BEATER

By timing purchases and sales at year-end, the cash method can save you tax.

The cash method is a simple way of keeping track of your income and in many cases can provide an opportunity to legally manipulate your profit. By making purchases at the end of the year and claiming the expense, you reduce income and you reduce your current year's tax liability. But beware, this is often a one-time deferral and once you have started this process, you will find yourself having to continue making purchases at the end of each year to delay the payment of tax.

EXAMPLE OF DEFERRING INCOME UNDER THE CASH ACCOUNTING METHOD

First let's assume the following:

	Year 1	Year 2
Sales	$50,000	$50,000
Other expenses	(20,000)	(20,000)
Thus, your profit:	$30,000	$30,000

Now let's assume that at the end of Year 1 you decide you will purchase all of next year's supplies this year. What happens?

	Year 1	Year 2
Sales	$50,000	$50,000
Other expenses		
including supplies	(20,000)	(20,000)
Adjustment for Year 2		
supplies purchased in Year 1	(2,000)	2,000
Total Expense	(22,000)	(18,000)
Net Profit	$28,000	$32,000

In the example, since you purchased Year 2 supplies in Year 1, "other expenses" in Year 2 is reduced by $2,000 because no supplies were purchased. To avoid this income inclusion, you need to purchase Year 3 supplies in Year 2. This will reduce Year 2 profit to $30,000. As can be seen, if you want to avoid the catch-up in one year, once you start prepaying expenses or delaying revenue, you will need to keep doing it into the future.

What Is the Accrual Accounting Method?

Accrual accounting sounds menacing, a term to be used only by professionals for the purpose of keeping their trade a secret. But really, accrual accounting is not complicated. The main principle behind accrual accounting is matching—making sure that revenues are reported in the same year as their related expenses.

For example, say you received an order to perform a service for a customer and you purchased the supplies and conducted the service before the year-end of your business. You billed your customer in the current year but they did not pay your bill until the next year. You have done everything relating to that sale except collect the money. To match the revenue with the expenses, accrual accounting tells us to record the revenue in the current year when it was earned and not in the second year, the year the money was received.

If you were to record the revenue on the sale in the next year when you received the money, you would have the expense in one year and the revenue in the next. The expense would not be matched with the revenue.

The same principle works in reverse. At the end of the year you purchase an item on credit from your supplier. You in turn sell the item and collect the money before the end of the year. Accrual accounting tells us to record the expense of purchasing that item in the current year even though you have not paid for it yet. You match the expense with the revenue.

From this, two general rules can be developed that will assist you in recording your business transactions:

Rule 1: Report the income of the business when it is earned, regardless of when you receive it.

Rule 2: Report the expenses of the business when they are incurred, regardless of when you actually pay the expense.

Do I Have to Use Accrual Accounting throughout the Year?

The simplest method of recording the transactions of your business is by using the cash basis. Report the transactions of your business as you receive the money or pay the expense. And provided you are not relying on monthly financial statements and your operations are relatively small, I recommend that you record your transactions this way throughout the year.

However, the Canada Revenue Agency will require that you report your income on the accrual basis, unless you meet one of the exceptions mentioned earlier. So, at the end of the year make an adjustment to your records to make them conform with accrual accounting principles.

The typical adjustments required to convert your cash basis records to accrual basis would be as follows:

Start with your income as reported under the cash basis

+   add to this the amount your customers still owed you at the end of the year

−   subtract from this the amount your customers still owed you at the end of last year

−   subtract from this the purchases which were made during the year but have not yet been paid for

+   add to this the purchases which were made last year but were not paid for at the end of last year

+   add to this the value of your inventory of goods on hand at the end of the year

−   and finally subtract from this the value of your inventory of goods on hand at the end of last year

EXAMPLE OF CONVERTING A CASH-BASED RECORD-KEEPING SYSTEM TO AN ACCRUAL-BASED SYSTEM

Income		$40,000
Add current accounts receivable	+	2,000
Subtract last year's accounts receivable	−	1,400
Subtract current accounts payable	−	2,500
Add last year's accounts payable	+	1,200
Add this year's inventory value	+	10,000
Subtract last year's inventory value	−	9,000
Accrual Income		$40,300

These are the most common adjustments for converting your cash-based accounting system to an accrual-based accounting system for small businesses. Depending on your operations, other adjustments may be required.

This procedure will create an accrual basis income or loss figure. From this you will then need to deduct such things as home-office expenses (see Round 8) and Capital Cost Allowance (see Round 9). This will then provide you with the income figure to be reported on your tax return.

You should note however that if you are registered for GST/HST and you are required to file your GST/HST returns either monthly or quarterly, then for the purposes of completing these returns you would have to use accrual accounting. What this means is that you have to remit the GST/HST on your invoices at the time you issue the invoice, not at the time when you collect the money on the invoice, as would be the case under cash basis of accounting. Similarly, you are entitled to claim an input tax credit on your purchases at the time you make the purchase, not necessarily the time you pay the account. For more information on the GST/HST see round six.

Start with the End in Mind

Choosing a year-end for your unincorporated business was once an easy task. Generally, if your business was profitable, a January or February year-end was usually chosen to defer income and the payment of taxes for one year. If your business was losing money, a November or December year-end was preferred to speed up the deduction of your losses.

On February 27, 1995, the federal government put an end to that planning. In their February budget and subsequent amendments, the government reduced or eliminated the advantages of a non-December year-end. This round will look at how this legislation affects you if you are choosing a year-end. Tax savings are still possible but the rules are complicated and you may have to rely on your tax coach if you hope to win Round 3 and "Beat the Taxman."

Must I Have a December Year-End?

Unless you are in a partnership and one of your partners is another partnership or a corporation, or worse still if your partnership has an interest in another partnership (I warned you this was complicated), then you still have the choice of having a non-December year-end. If you choose a non-December year-end you must file an election with your personal income tax return.

Why Would I Want a Non-December Year-End?

Tax savings! Tax savings! Tax savings! If your business is profitable, a non-December year-end can still provide you with tax savings by deferring income into the future. Tax deferrals are available in years where the income from your business is increasing. For this reason it may make sense for you to file the prescribed elections and choose a non-December year-end.

Should I Have a December or a Non-December Year-End?

TAX BEATER

Speed up tax savings by choosing a December year-end when your business is losing money during the early years.

TAX BEATER

Defer tax by staying with a non-December year-end if your income is increasing.

Whether or not you should operate your business with a December year-end or some other year-end is an individual decision which only you can make with some assistance from your tax coach. However, here are some factors you may want to consider:

- If you are just starting a new business and it is losing money, you may want to pick a December year-end to speed up the claiming of the losses which can be used to reduce the tax you will pay on other sources of income.

- Generally, if your ongoing business is growing and the income that you are reporting on your tax return is increasing, a non-December year-end will provide a small tax deferral. For example, if your year-end is January, you will include in income an amount pro-rated based on your January income. If your income is increasing, you will always report a lesser amount with a January year-end than with a December year-end.

- Generally, if your ongoing business is in decline and the income that you are reporting on your tax return is decreasing, switching to a December year-end will save you tax dollars. By having a non-December year-end when your income is dropping, you will be in effect prepaying tax. Switching to a December year-end will stop this from occurring.

- Once you change or start to report on a December year-end basis, you cannot elect back to a non-December year-end. So if you decide you are going to go to a December year-end, make sure that this is the right decision for you, as there is no going back.

- When starting out in a business, if you have significant income from other sources and the business income would be taxed at the highest rate in the first year, consider a non-December year-end to defer the tax liability for a year. However, make sure you plan for the taxes that will become due.

- Overall, December year-ends provide the fewest hassles and frustrations. Having a non-December year-end creates many complexities. If there is very little tax benefit to having a non-December year-end, moving to December is usually in your best interest.

TAX BEATER
Save tax by changing to a December year-end if income from an established business is decreasing.

What Happens If I Elect to Have a Non-December Year-End?

If you elect to keep a January year-end, for example, you can continue to complete the year-end of your business for accounting purposes on a February to January basis. However, for tax purposes you will be required to mathematically convert your January year-end to a December year-end.

The conversion to a December year-end is done by multiplying your January year-end profit by the number of days remaining in the calendar year that you operated your business divided by the total number of days in the fiscal year you operated your business. The result of this calculation is then added to your January year-end profit and last year's calculation is subtracted, to give an estimated December profit figure.

For example, assume that your January year-end profit was $50,000. To arrive at your deemed December year-end profit figure you would multiply the $50,000 by 334 days remaining in the calendar year divided by 365 days in the fiscal year of your business. This works out to $45,753. You add the $45,753 to the $50,000 January year-end profit and then subtract the similar calculation that was done in the prior year. If in the prior year your January profit figure was $40,000, then you subtract $36,603 ($40,000 x 334 days ÷ 365 days). The result is that the income you include on your tax return is not the $50,000 your business earned up until January, but instead $59,150 ($50,000 + $45,753 − $36,603).

What If This Is My First Year in Business?

If this is your first year in business and you decide to have a non-December year-end, you may be faced with some very significant cash flow problems if you don't plan properly. In the first year that you report business income, if you have a non-December year-end you must mathematically calculate your income as if you had a December year-end. As described above, if your business had a January year-end and you started your business on February 1 of the previous year, this would mean taking your January profit and multiplying it by 334 days divided by 365 days. However, you would not be able to subtract from this anything for the previous year, as this is the first year of operations. Therefore, in the above example, your income inclusion would be $50,000 plus $45,753 or $95,753.

Remember that the 365 days in the above example represents the number of days in your fiscal year. If, for example, you started your business May 1 and chose a January 31 year-end, the calculation to work out your business income would be $50,000 plus $50,000 x 334 ÷ 276 = $60,507 or $110,507.

By choosing a non-December year-end you have deferred income in the first year, but instead of this deferral continuing for as long as you are in business, as under the old rules, the deferral catches up to you all at once in the next year. If you don't plan for this, you may find yourself having a difficult time paying your tax liability.

Had you picked a December year-end, approximately the same amount of income would have been reported; however, the income would have been spread over two years. With the income being paid over two years, cash flow may be less of a problem and the leveling of the income will make better use of the lower tax rates. Leveling the income out over two years in comparison to having all of the income being reported in one year will save you tax and provide that knockout punch we're all looking for.

The table below shows a comparison of tax payments due on a calendar and a non-calendar year-end assuming a constant $50,000 level of income over three years.

COMPARISON OF TAX PAYMENTS DUE ON A CALENDAR AND NON-CALENDAR YEAR-END

	Calendar Year-End $	Non-Calendar Year-End $
Year 1		
Tax Paid in Year 1	Nil	Nil
Year 2		
April 30 Tax Paid for Year 1	16,000	Nil
September 15 Instalment for Year 2	8,000	Nil
December 15 Instalment for Year 2	8,000	Nil
Tax Paid in Year 2	32,000	Nil

Year 3

March 15 Instalment for Year 3	4,000	Nil
April 30 Tax Paid for Year 2	0	39,100
June 15 Instalment for Year 3	4,000	Nil
September 15 Instalment for Year 3	4,000	8,000*
December 15 Instalment for Year 3	4,000	8,000*
Tax Paid in Year 3	16,000	55,100
Total Tax Paid Over Years 1, 2 and 3	48,000	55,100

Assumptions:
- Taxpayer has no other sources of income, and is single
- Taxpayer's income is constant at $50,000 per year
- Federal and typical provincial tax rates used, rounded to nearest hundred. Rates will vary from province to province.

* The taxpayer would elect to make the minimum instalment required expecting that next year's income will be $50,000. (See Round 7.)

As can be seen in the above table, despite the fact that it is assumed that the business income is $50,000 per year under both alternatives, having a non-calendar year-end resulted in an additional $7,100 tax owing over the initial three years of the business. This is caused by the fact that with a non-calendar year-end, you end up having two years of income being taxed all at once. This results in a lot of income being taxed at the highest tax level. The more you can equalize your income from year-to-year, maximize your lower tax levels and minimize income being taxed at the higher tax levels, the less tax you will pay. This will be discussed more in Round 4.

How Can I Minimize the Non-December Year-End Tax Problems?

The tax and cash flow problems described above occur because two years of income are included on one year's tax return. To minimize this potential tax problem, the government will allow you to elect to include an amount of income in the first year of operations. This income inclusion can be any amount between zero and the actual business income reported in your first fiscal year times the number of days you carried on business in your first calendar year, divided by the number of days in your first fiscal period.

For example, assume you started your business on March 1, 2008, and you have chosen a January 31, 2009, year-end. You have no other income in 2008 and your business income for the period ending January 31, 2009, was $50,000. Your income options for 2008 and 2009 are as follows:

Option 1

In 2008, do not elect to include any business income and therefore pay no tax for your 2008 tax return. In 2009 your income will be $50,000 plus $50,000 times 334 days remaining in the 2009 calendar year divided by 337 days that you operated your business in the first year, or $99,555.

Option 2

You elect to include the maximum amount of business income in 2008. The maximum amount of business income is $50,000 times the number of days you operated your business in 2008, or 306 days, divided by the number of days you operated your business in its first fiscal year, or 337. The maximum amount you would be able to claim on your 2008 tax return would be $45,400.

> **TAX BEATER**
> Elect to include income in your first year of business to reduce income taxed at high tax rates.

In 2009, the income you report on your tax return would be the $50,000 plus $49,555 ($50,000 x 334 ÷ 337) minus $45,400 ($50,000 x 306 ÷ 337) or $54,155.

Option 3

You elect to include on your 2008 personal tax return business income within the range of zero to $45,400, as calculated above.

This ability to elect an amount to include in income does provide some flexibility in tax planning in the early stages of your business. However, the tax planning is short lived, for whatever you don't include in the first year, you will have to include in income in the second year.

Where this flexibility can be useful, though, is if the excess income is at the same tax level in both years. By electing to include in 2008 only enough income to bring your taxable income up to the highest tax level and deferring the balance until next year, you will then provide maximum tax savings and also provide a tax deferral. Deferring the balance into the next year can provide an even greater punch in this climate of reducing tax rates.

TAX BEATER

Elect to defer income that will be taxed in the current year at the highest tax rate.

When Can I Choose a December Year-End?

At any time, you can switch to a December year-end for your business. By switching, you can avoid all of the hassles and headaches of calculating each year your income inclusion under the non-December year-end format.

Be forewarned, however, that once you switch, there is no turning back. Once you have decided to go with a December year-end and file your tax return in that manner, the Canada Revenue Agency will not allow you to later change back to a non-December year-end. So consider talking this over with your tax coach before making the switch.

What Year-End Should I Choose for My Corporation?

Deciding on a year-end for a corporation is considerably easier than for a sole proprietorship or partnership. The government will allow a corporation to have a non-December year-end without requiring the company to recalculate it's profit as if the company had a December year-end. There are no stub periods and no additional income calculations. The only limit on picking a year-end is that you cannot pick a year-end that is longer than 53 weeks from the date of incorporation. The determination of a corporations year-end is usually decided by two factors, business and tax.

Depending on your business, there may be a month or time of the year that would be more logical than other times of the year to have a year-end. Many retail stores have January as a year-end as the store inventory is usually at the lowest point after the Christmas rush and boxing day sales. Whereas the summer months might be a good time of the year for a year-end for a ski or winter resort. With a corporation you can easily pick the month that works best for your business.

The other factor to consider is tax. With corporations, there are a few tax advantages that can be obtained by picking one month over another month for your year-end. If your business is profitable, then the general rule of thumb is that you are going to want to pick a year-end that is the closest to twelve months from incorporation in order to delay as long as possible the tax you will have to pay on that profit. On the other hand, if your business is losing money or breaking even, you may want to a pick a year-end earlier or at the end of the month that your business starts to make money. This will then also defer tax for as long as possible. However, these tax deferrals are very short lived and only occur in the first year.

In addition, having a fall year-end for a corporation can provide some tax planning flexibility when looking at the salary remuneration of the owner. This is discussed in more detail in Round 4, the corporate income-splitting technique. Overall, however, if there is a strong business reason for a certain year-end, then often this business reason will make the determination.

The Tax Rate Stairway: Easy Steps to Saving Money

Understanding how you pay income taxes is key to reducing the amount of tax you pay. In Canada, the income tax system is designed so that, generally, the more money you make, the higher you climb on the tax rate stairway, resulting in more tax that you will pay to the government. This concept is often referred to as the Marginal Tax Rate system, but I like to call it the Tax Rate Stairway, since marginal tax brackets look a lot like stairs in a staircase.

There are five main tax steps or levels. The first tax level has a tax rate of 0%. (Technically the tax rate is approximately 25%. However, as all individuals are entitled to a basic personal exemption of $9,600, the effective tax rate is 0%.) This rate is applied on income from $0 to the level of your personal tax credit, which for most is $9,600. This personal exemption, as well as the various tax levels are indexed to inflation. The second tax level has an approximate tax rate of 25% (including provincial taxes) and is assessed on taxable income between $9,600 and $37,885. The next $37,884 of taxable income, that is income between $37,884 and $75,769, is taxed at a rate of approximately 35%. The next

$47,415 of taxable income, that is income between $74,769 and $123,184, is taxed at a rate of about 42%. The balance, or income in excess of $123,184, is taxed at around 46%. Tax rates vary from province to province with Nova Scotia having the highest maximum personal tax rate of 48.25% and Alberta having the lowest maximum personal tax rate of 39% for 2008.

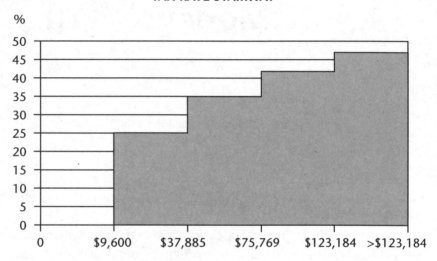

TAX RATE STAIRWAY

How Do I Use the Tax Rate Stairway to Save?

A key to saving taxes is understanding that when your income moves from a lower tax level to a higher tax level, only the increase in income is taxed at the higher rate. For example, say Jane has $39,000 of taxable income. The first $9,600 of taxable income will not be taxed, the next $28,285 will be taxed at about 25%, and the additional $1,115 will be taxed at approximately 35%. Just because Jane has jumped to the third tax level, it doesn't mean that all of her income is taxed at that rate—just the income in excess of $37,885.

Your tax planning objective is to maximize your use of the lower tax levels whenever possible. Poor tax planning occurs when you don't take advantage of the rules that allow you to

TAX BEATER

Maximize income in lower tax levels and minimize income in higher tax levels.

even out your income from year to year and to avoid those "dreaded" high tax levels.

For example, assume that in Year 1 you have taxable income of $110,000. In Year 2 this drops to $10,000. By averaging your income out to, say, $60,000 for both years, you could save up to $7,000 in tax.

SAVE TAX BY LEVELING YOUR INCOME FROM YEAR-TO-YEAR

	Alt 1	Alt 2
	$	$
Year 1 Taxable Income	110,000	60,000
Year 2 Taxable Income	10,000	60,000
Taxable Income for the 2 Years	120,000	120,000
Tax Paid Over the 2 Years	34,600	27,600
Tax Saved by Leveling Income		**7,000**

Note: Calculations based on no other income, only personal credit claimed and Ontario provincial tax rates used. Effects on CPP have been ignored. Rates and tax savings will vary from province to province.

Similar tax savings can be realized by leveling the income of the family. For example, instead of having one spouse report $110,000 a year in income and the other spouse report $10,000, if both spouses could report $60,000 a year in income the family income would be the same, however the family tax bill would be lower by approximately $7,000. A significant savings for using the tax rate stairway to your best advantage.

What Are the Income-Splitting Techniques?

Now, I recognize that we do not live in a perfect world where we can dictate exactly what our income should be in order to maximize our tax savings. Life should be so easy. But there are many legitimate ways to shift income from one tax level to another. In fact, planning for the transfer of income from one level to another is one of the keys to tax planning.

There are three general techniques for transferring income from a higher tax level to a lower one. The first technique is *Family Income Splitting*. As the name suggests, family income splitting is accomplished by transferring income between family members and maximizing the lower tax levels. This can be done through the use of RRSPs, loans, and salaries.

The second technique is *Personal Income Splitting*. Personal income splitting is accomplished by transferring income from one year to the next on your own personal tax return and maximizing the lower tax levels in the process. This can be accomplished through the use of RRSPs, certain reserves, by applying losses to different years, and by timing discretionary expenses like capital cost allowance.

The third technique is *Corporate Income Splitting*. Corporate income splitting is accomplished by transferring income to a corporation. A corporation is taxed differently than an individual and, sometimes, at a lower tax rate. Maximizing the lower tax rates inside the corporation as well as the family's personal tax rates can result in significant tax savings.

We'll examine each of the three income-splitting techniques in more detail below.

The Family Income-Splitting Technique

The first and easiest technique for effective income splitting is to split income among your family members. With a small or home-based business, you can do this a number of ways. However, before I discuss the different methods, it is important that you understand "attribution" and how it can foil even the best laid plans.

What Is Attribution?

Recognizing that significant tax savings can be achieved by splitting income among family members, the government has legislated a number of rules to stop people from arbitrarily allocating income between family members. These are known as the attribution rules.

For example, Mrs. Jones gifts money to her spouse to invest and earn investment income. Because her spouse has never worked and has never had a source of income, the investment income earned is attributed back to Mrs. Jones and taxed in her hands at her tax rate. This income-splitting technique is denied because gifts made between spouses or minor children for the purpose of investing and earning investment income fall into the attribution rules.

> **TAX BEATER**
>
> Save significant tax dollars by legally allocating income among family members.

Can I Lend My Spouse or Children Money To Invest?

If you have the only source of income for the family and you lend money to your spouse or minor child to invest and thereby make use of the tax savings available through family income splitting, Canada Revenue Agency will require you, not your spouse or your children, to report the investment income. There are however some exceptions to this general rule.

- If you lend money to your spouse or minor child and charge interest at the government's prescribed interest rate in effect at the time of setting up the loan, then the investment income earned on the investment will not be attributed back to yourself. (See page 109 for more information on prescribed interest rates.) Your spouse or child will get a tax deduction for the interest paid to you and you will have to report the interest as income. If the investments return more than the interest rate charged, then as a family, tax can be saved. With interest rates being relatively low, this can result in some significant tax savings. Remember, however, to ensure that the interest is actually paid within 30 days after the end of the year or by January 30th. If the interest is not actually paid, then the deal is off and the investment income will be attributed back to you.

> **TAX BEATER**
>
> Lend money to your spouse or minor child at a prescribed interest rate and save tax dollars.

- Second generation investment income is not attributed back to the lender. Second generation income is investment income earned on investment income. The problem with this planning strategy is that it is often very difficult to track the second generation income and unless you are fortunate to be dealing with very large numbers, the tax savings are often not significant enough to warrant all of the time needed to track it. However, for some this is a very effective income-splitting tool.

TAX BEATER

Invest money lent to children in capital gain producing assets and avoid attribution.

- Loans to minor children where the money is used to invest in capital gain producing assets will avoid attribution. If you lend money to your minor child interest free, and that money is used to generate capital gains, the capital gains will be taxed in your child's hands not yours. This unique exception for minor children can provide significant tax savings to the family. However, be careful because capital gain producing investments are generally more risky than interest producing investments. Make sure this risk is acceptable to you and your family.

TAX BEATER

Invest child tax benefit receipts in the name of your child and save tax dollars.

- Income earned from child tax benefit receipts from the government invested in your child's name will not be attributed back to yourself. This has been a long concession made by the government in that money received under the old family allowance system and now under the child tax benefit system could be invested by minor children and the income could be reported by them. This can over time, shelter significant amounts of income from tax.

Can I Lend My Spouse Money to Start a Small or Home-Based Business?

Another exception to the attribution rules that succeeds in splitting income between family members is a non-interest bearing business loan. If you wish to start a business and your spouse has the means to provide you with a loan to help you get started or supplement the operations, then no attribution will occur on the income from the business.

This means that the income earned in the business will be taxed in your hands. The business income will not be added to your spouse's tax return. This result is due to the fact that loans made between spouses or minor children for the purpose of operating a business do not fall into the attribution rules.

TAX BEATER

Lending money to a family member to finance a small or home-based business is allowable income splitting.

Can I Pay a Member of My Family a Salary?

An effective method of splitting income with family members is to pay your spouse, child, or parent a salary. A "reasonable" salary paid to your family member will be tax deductible from your business, thereby reducing your tax liability. The salary will be declared as income on your family member's tax return and could be taxed at a much lower level on the tax rate stairway, if it is taxed at all. Be aware, there are restrictions on the salary that you pay to a family member (see "Are There Limits to the Salary I Can Pay to My Family?" on page 47).

Children

Income splitting by paying a teenage child a salary can be extremely advantageous. For example, assume your teenage son or daughter does not have a part-time job but wishes to start saving for post-secondary school or needs money for car insurance, clothing, entertainment, etc. Consider putting them on the payroll rather than just giving them the money.

By putting them on the payroll of your business, you can get a tax deduction for the money you were going to give them anyway, and if the income is less than their personal exemption rate of $9,600, they won't pay any income tax at all. Depending on your circumstances, this could result in an annual tax savings of about $3,700 per year, per child. It is important to remember that the salary must be reasonable and for work actually performed by your son or daughter.

TAX BEATER

Save as much as $3,700 per child, per year, by putting your children on salary.

SAVE TAX BY PAYING YOUR CHILD A SALARY

	Alt 1 (No Salary to Child) $	Alt 2 (Salary to Child) $
Entrepreneur's Taxable Income	130,000	122,000
Child's Taxable Income	0	8,000
Taxable Income for Parent & Child	130,000	130,000
Tax Paid by Both	43,500	39,800
Tax Saved by Paying Your Child a Salary		**3,700**

Note: Calculations based on no other income, only personal credit claimed and Ontario provincial tax rates used. Effects on CPP have been ignored. Rates and tax savings will vary from province to province.

Now that your children are on the payroll, don't forget to ensure they file a personal tax return. There are several reasons for filing tax returns, even if their income is too low to pay tax. First, filing a tax return helps to support that they received this income. It completes the paper trail. You have cheques showing the wages paid, T4's were completed to report the income, and your children filed tax returns reporting this income for the year.

Secondly, filing a tax return establishes RRSP contribution room. Eighteen percent of earned income, which includes employment and business income, up to a maximum of $20,000 ($21,000 for 2009), can be contributed into an RRSP in the following year (less various adjustments for contributions into a Registered Pension Plan). If you don't make an RRSP contribution, the amount you could have contributed just carries forward and gets added to next years calculation. Under the current rules, the unused contribution room has no limit and can be carried forward indefinitely, or at least until you can no longer contribute to an RRSP due to your age. Therefore, filing a tax return will build a future tax savings vehicle for your children.

You may want to consider going one step further and actually have your children make a contribution to their RRSP, but not deduct the contribution. Given that their income will likely be below $9,600 and therefore not taxable, there is no immediate tax advantage to making the contribution. The non-deducted contribution can be carried forward just like the contribution room. However, it does get them started early in saving for their retirement, which could, due to compounding, result in a significant portfolio when they retire. You may not want to consider this however, if you feel there may be some risk that your children would not be able to deduct the RRSP in the future due to illness or possibility they may not have any source of income.

> **TAX BEATER**
> File tax returns for your children and build RRSP contribution room.

Parent

Less common, but equally effective, is paying a salary to your parent(s). If their income is low and you wish to assist them financially, consider paying them a salary out of your business as opposed to just giving them the money. This can reduce income taxes by providing you with a tax deduction at your higher income tax rate and having it taxed in the hands of your parent at a lower rate. By maximizing the lower tax rates in your family as a whole, you will pay less tax overall. Again, remember the salary must be reasonable for the work performed.

> **TAX BEATER**
> Pay a dependent parent a salary.

Spouse

Last, but certainly not least, you should consider paying a salary to your spouse. For all the support he or she has provided you, it is the least you can do. However, the savings may not be as great as with a teenage son or daughter.

If your spouse has no other source of income, then you will already be claiming him or her as a dependant and receiving a tax credit on your tax return for approximately 25% of $9,600. If your taxable income, which includes the income from the business, is $37,885 or less, then there is no significant tax advantage to paying your spouse a salary. A tax deduction on your tax return at 25% will only be replaced with a tax liability on your spouse's return at 25% or a reduction in the marriage amount at 25%. No real tax advantage is obtained and there may even be a cost with this strategy.

TAX BEATER

If your income is in excess of $37,885 and your spouse is in a lower bracket, pay your spouse a salary.

However, if your income is taxed above 25%, then you can achieve real tax savings by paying your spouse a salary. If your business is making, say, $50,000, then paying your spouse a salary of $10,000 can "Beat the Taxman" for about $900 annually. You can achieve even greater savings if your income is being taxed at the highest tax level. See the chart below for details on how this is calculated.

SAVE TAX BY PAYING YOUR SPOUSE A SALARY

	Alt 1 (No Salary to Spouse) $	Alt 2 (Salary to Spouse) $
Entrepreneur's Taxable Income	50,000	40,000
Spouse's Taxable Income	10,000	20,000
Taxable Income for Couple	60,000	60,000
Tax Paid by Couple	10,900	10,000
Tax Saved by Paying Your Spouse a Salary		900

Note: Calculations based on no other income, only personal credit claimed and typical provincial tax rates used. Effects on CPP have been ignored. Rates will vary from province to province.

The key to this type of planning is to keep in mind the tax rate stairway. Tax savings are obtained from reducing the amount of income that is taxed at high income rates and increasing the amount taxed at lower rates. If both you and your spouse are in the same income tax level, or if your spouse is in a higher income tax level, then it won't make sense to pay them a salary. In these cases, this tax reduction technique is not for you.

Are There Limits to the Salary I Can Pay to My Family?

It is very important to recognize that the salary paid must be reasonable in the circumstances. It would not be reasonable to pay your two-year-old child a salary to reduce income taxes unless this child is actually contributing to the operations of your business. Salaries should not be paid out just to reduce income taxes. You should be able to provide business reasons as to why the particular individual deserves a salary, evidence that the individual actually did work, and that the salary paid is an amount that you would normally pay a stranger.

If you do not take care in paying reasonable salaries for services rendered, you will run the risk of having the tax deduction denied. As well, Canada Revenue Agency may assess an additional penalty of taxing the salary in the hands of the family member. This "double taxation" does get applied occasionally. In addition, you will be charged interest on the tax liability caused by the denial of the salary.

These penalties are rare in the case of providing salaries to family members. However, they can and have been assessed in cases where taxpayers have become too aggressive in their planning. This is one Round we definitely want to win so remember "reasonable salary for the work performed."

> **TAX BEATER**
> Salary for family members must be reasonable and for services rendered.

Does My Family Have to Pay Employment Insurance Premiums on Their Salary?

If you pay your spouse or other members of your family a salary, you must make the proper withholdings and remit these withholdings plus the employer's portion on time. In most cases, the amount being remitted will include income tax, and the employee's and employer's portion of CPP (Canada Pension Plan) and EI (Employment Insurance). However, it is likely that your spouse and/or your family members are exempt from EI. (EI, or employment insurance, used to be known as UI, or unemployment insurance.)

Under the general rules normally, only the owner of a business is exempt from EI. As an owner of a sole proprietorship, all of the profit or loss is yours to report as income or loss on your tax return. None of this profit is subject to contributions to the Employment Insurance plan.

With a corporation, any shareholder who owns more than 40% of the voting shares of the company can be exempt from having to pay EI. So, if your business is incorporated and you own 100% of the shares, you will not have to pay EI on any salary paid to you out of the company.

However, if you hire your spouse, either within an incorporated business or in a sole proprietorship, you should not have to withhold EI from his or her pay. This would also apply to a salary paid to any other family member.

You can be exempt from paying EI on a family member's salary if the family member acts less as a regular employee and more like an owner of the business or some special relationship. Since your family members are related to you, if their activities in the business resemble those of an owner or some special relationship not offered to other employees, then family members can be exempt from paying EI and the business will not have to pay the employer's portion.

The logic here is that the government will not pay EI to family members who are laid off if they had a relationship with the business that was unique as compared to any other employee. On the other hand, if the family member's relationship with the company is very similar to any other employee's relationship, then the family member would likely be eligible for EI benefits. Human Resources Development Canada (HRDC) decides who gets EI benefits and who does not. However, Canada Revenue Agency (CRA) determines which employee relationships are covered under the EI plan, which will affect an employee's right to a benefit. So, if you want to know if you must withhold EI from a family member's salary, the question should be directed to CRA. After all, there is no sense in paying into the EI plan if your family is not going to be eligible to collect from the plan.

To find out if your family members should be exempt from EI, you can request a ruling be made by CRA. Contact your local CRA office and ask for Form CPT 1, "Request For A Ruling As To The Status Of A Worker Under The Canada Pension Plan and/or Employment Insurance Act." This form is to be used by the employer to determine the status of the employee relationship. There is another form, CPT 2, which is used by the employee to request a ruling about their relationship with their employer. As the employer, you should use form CPT 1. Complete this form and submit it to CRA. They should respond within a reasonable time frame with their ruling. If the ruling is favourable for you, then you can accept their ruling and abide by it. On the other hand, if the ruling is unfavourable, then you can appeal the ruling and if necessary take their ruling to court.

TAX BEATER

Apply to have your family member EI exempt.

When making these rulings, what the government is looking for is whether or not the terms and conditions of employment of your family member is substantially the same as the terms and conditions of employment that would reasonably be offered to other employees. Specifically, Canada Revenue Agency looks at a number of factors, including:

- The remuneration paid (e.g., how and when is the worker paid and on what basis);

- The terms of employment (e.g., hours of work, duties);

- The duration of work performed; and

- The nature and importance of work performed.

It is important to note, that with family members, the general presumption is that EI will not need to be withheld and paid into the plan because they will not normally be eligible for EI benefits. However, if you would like your family member to be eligible for EI benefits then you can request a ruling.

If you have been paying EI for your family members over the past number of years and you have obtained a ruling stating you are not required to withhold EI, you can request a refund of the EI for the past three years. To apply for this refund, ask the Canada Revenue Agency for the form PD24(E), "Application For a Refund of Overdeducted CPP Contributions or EI Premiums." Complete this form and submit it along with a completed Form CPT 1 ruling request.

TAX BEATER

Apply for refunds of EI paid to family members for up to three prior years.

Canada Revenue Agency will review the PD24(E) form and your ruling request. If accepted, Canada Revenue Agency will refund to the employer the portion of the employment insurance contribution that was paid. Canada Revenue Agency will also automatically amend the employee's personal tax returns for the years requested and refund the EI that was withheld from their pay. In some businesses, this has meant thousands of tax dollars refunded.

What About Making Members of My Family Partners?

Paying a salary to a family member provides the most flexible means of income splitting. If the business is doing well, then it may be possible to adjust the family salaries upwards to maximize the lower tax levels. On the other hand, if the business is not doing that well, the salaries can be adjusted downward. However, the payment of salaries can be an administrative headache.

If your business does not have other employees, placing family members on the payroll will require you to obtain payroll account numbers and to remit withholding taxes, Canada Pension Plan or Quebec Pension Plan contributions, and possibly Employment Insurance contributions. Additionally, depending on the province and the circumstances, you may need to make Workers Compensation and Employers Health Tax payments. It is for these reasons that you should take care to ensure that you achieve substantial savings with your income splitting technique so that the tax savings outweigh the administrative costs.

A simpler method of income splitting with a family member is to go into partnership with the family member. In this case, both or all of the members of the family are owners of the business; therefore, the payroll issues are eliminated. However, in most cases, the profit or loss from the business must be allocated based on a predetermined arrangement, and it is difficult to reasonably adjust this allocation from year-to-year. (This is discussed in more detail in Round 5, "To Incorporate or Not.")

Making your spouse or other family members partners also means giving up partial ownership of the business. There can be many drawbacks to sharing ownership that may make this alternative not acceptable. However, in many cases, the partnership structure will provide the income splitting desired without the additional costs and headaches involved in having a payroll.

TAX BEATER

If you do not already have employees, con-sider making your family member(s) partners. This avoids costs and headaches involved in having a payroll.

How Do I Use RRSPs for Family Income-Splitting

RRSPs can also be used as a family income-splitting technique. Spousal contributions can maximize your tax deductions today and defer and transfer income to your spouse to be taxed in your retirement years at his or her lower tax levels.

Spousal contributions work by providing the contributor with a tax deduction on his or her tax return. However, since the contribution was made into a spouse's RRSP plan, the non-contributing spouse will report the RRSP in his or her income when the money is taken out.

If you plan to make use of this technique, be careful. There are several rules and objectives to keep in mind when contributing to spousal RRSPs.

First of all, remember that the objective with spousal contributions is to maximize both your own and your spouse's lower income levels when you retire. So you want to build both your own and your spouse's retirement accounts for maximum benefit. If your spouse is likely to be receiving a pension on retirement then spousal contributions may not be for you. On the other hand, if neither of you is going to receive a company pension, both of your RRSP accounts should grow in equal amounts to maximize the use of lower tax levels when you retire.

You must also remember that you must stop making spousal RRSP contributions for three years before your spouse starts withdrawing the contributions unless one of the following situations applies: the RRSP is transferred into an RRIF and no more than the minimum amount is withdrawn, or you become separated from your spouse. There are also special rules if you or your spouse pass away. If you do not stop making RRSP contributions for three years to any spousal plan before your spouse starts withdrawal, the RRSP withdrawal will be included in your income, not your spouse's. These rules apply even if you make spousal contributions to different plans.

TAX BEATER

Make spousal RRSP contributions to save taxes today and tomorrow.

The Personal Income-Splitting Technique

Personal income-splitting is more difficult than family income-splitting. As discussed earlier, what I refer to as the personal income-splitting technique is the transferring of your income from one taxation year to a different year, leveling your personal income in the process. Canada Revenue Agency is reluctant to amend prior years' tax returns to perform what is referred to as retroactive tax planning. So instead of amending prior years' returns to maximize the lower tax levels, you must conduct your affairs in such a way as to maximize these lower levels today and into the future. Although more difficult, with a little bit of careful planning, this can still be done effectively.

Why Would I Not Deduct RRSP Contributions?

One effective method of personal income splitting is to delay the deduction of your RRSP contributions. This method can be effective in years where your income is low. For example, assume that in year one your business is not doing very well and your income is being taxed in the lowest tax level of 25%. However, early indications for next year are that your business will be very profitable and you will have income taxed at 46%. By holding off deducting your RRSP contribution until next year, you can get an additional 21% in tax savings from this deduction.

This tax saving occurs because RRSP contributions are treated as a tax deduction, with the tax savings being based on your tax level. If you are in a 25% tax level, for every dollar you contribute to an RRSP, you will save 25 cents. If you are in a 46% tax level, for every dollar you contribute to an RRSP, you will save 46 cents.

Note that in our example the recommendation is to hold off *deducting* the RRSP contribution on your tax return, not to hold off *making* the contribution. For many reasons you should make an RRSP contribution every year. Remember, income earned in the RRSP is not subject to tax until you withdraw the money. So, you can get up to a 46% tax savings with your contribution plus a tax-deferred return on the money invested. If your next year's income is expected to be low, simply defer deducting your contribution to a high-income year.

> **TAX BEATER**
>
> Hold off deducting your RRSP contribution in a year where your income is low and you expect next year's income to be high.

How Can I Make Money When My Business Lost Money?

OK, you had a bad year, and your business lost money. It happens. Even some of the biggest corporations lose money occasionally. It's nothing to be ashamed of. But don't compound your bad luck by not filing your tax return. Make sure you use your business loss to get money back from the government.

Taxpayers sometimes make the unfortunate mistake of thinking that since they lost money, they will have no taxes to pay and don't bother to complete a tax return. As a result, they end up paying too much tax. Despite all of our good income-splitting ideas, not filing your tax return is a sure way to lose Round 4.

Business losses are one of the most flexible personal income-splitting techniques because you can deduct the losses over any of the past three years or the next twenty years, if your loss occurs in 2006 or a later taxation year. Note that if your loss occurs in a taxation year ending after March 22, 2004 and before 2006, the loss may be carried forward for 10 years. If your loss occurs before March 22, 2004, you can deduct the loss only over the subsequent seven years.

How Do I Calculate My Loss?

If your business lost money in the current year, you may be able to deduct this from income earned in other tax years. But first, you must calculate your eligible loss.

Your first step is to calculate your business loss and enter it on your tax return. Then add in all of your other sources of income, like investment income, pension income, etc. From this, subtract your eligible deductions from income, like carrying charges.

If, after recording all of this information, the taxable income on your tax return is a negative, you will have a loss that can be used to reduce taxes you have paid or will pay.

Note that just because your business lost money, it does not necessarily mean you have a loss which you can carry-forward or carry-back. You must first deduct your business loss from all other sources of income in the current year before you can carry any balance forward or back.

How Do I Carry a Loss Back or Forward?

Business losses can be carried back three years and carried forward twenty, if the loss arose in the 2006 or later taxation year. If the loss arose between March 22, 2004 and before 2006, it can be carried forward for a period of ten years, and if the loss arose in a tax year ending before March 22, 2004 then it can be carried forward for only seven years. If you want to carry the loss back to any of the three previous years, you must file an election with your current year's tax return. You need to complete Canada Revenue Agency form T1A, "Request For Loss Carry Back" and submit it with your tax return.

Technically, if you wish to carry a loss back, you must file the T1A form by the filing deadline of your current year's tax return. Administratively, Canada Revenue Agency will usually accept late-filed elections; however, there is no guarantee. To ensure that you save all the tax you are entitled to save, file the election on time.

> **TAX BEATER**
> Apply a loss to the third prior taxation year before it is too late.

To Which Years Should I Carry the Loss Back?

Deciding which year to apply the loss against is not a precise science and only time will tell if you've made the right choice. But if you do some proper planning, you can make a significant difference in the amount of your tax refund. Make sure you consider the following:

> **TAX BEATER**
> Apply a loss over the past three years to minimize higher income levels.

- If it appears that next year you will also have a loss, then consider carrying the loss back to the third previous year. You will never be able to carry a loss back to that particular year again.

- If you expect that this is the only year for a loss, look over your past three years and allocate the loss over the three years to minimize your high rate income. Keeping in mind that your tax-planning objective is to maximize the lower tax levels and minimize the higher tax levels, look over your past three tax returns and allocate enough of the loss to each of the years so that the revised taxable income maximizes the lower tax levels.

> **TAX BEATER**
> Carry losses forward if next year's income is expected to be high.

- If your income for the past three years has been relatively low and you expect that your income in future years will be higher, consider carrying the loss forward instead of applying it to prior tax years. The tax refund may not be as immediate, but if you are expecting income in the higher tax levels, the tax savings may be greater.

What Are Reserves?

A very effective method of saving tax through personal income-splitting is in the use of tax reserves. Tax reserves are legitimate ways of deferring income to a future year. And every time you can defer paying tax you save money.

Are There Any Reserves I Can Claim?

There are several different types of reserves, most only apply to specific industries or transactions. However, one reserve that a small-business entrepreneur is likely to encounter is for *services not rendered* or *goods undelivered*.

Assume that your customer pays you in advance to develop a program for their computer. Since you received the money for the job, you record it as a sale. However, by year-end, you haven't completed the job or delivered the product. Since the service hasn't been rendered or the goods haven't been delivered, you don't have to claim the income in this taxation year. You have effectively deferred revenue to the next year, reduced your tax liability, and scored another point in winning Round 4.

Another common reserve for small businesses is the *allowance for doubtful accounts* reserve. As discussed in Round 2, Canada Revenue Agency requires most businesses to use the accrual accounting method to report income. With this method, you must add to the business's income amounts that have been billed to your customers but not yet collected. Should you feel that one or more of your customers may not pay their bills, then you can claim a reserve for these doubtful accounts.

Claiming a reserve for doubtful accounts does not mean that you are writing off the account and have given up trying to collect the receivable. It does mean that in your best judgement there is doubt about the collectability of the account. This reserve allows you to pay tax on the income in the year you collect the money, not in the year you have made the sale.

TAX BEATER

Claim a reserve for income that has been received but in return for which services have not been rendered or goods have not been shipped.

TAX BEATER

Claim reserves on questionable receivables.

Should I Claim Capital Cost Allowance?

If you own capital assets that are used in your business, such as an automobile, furniture, or a computer, you may be faced with the question of whether or not to claim capital cost allowance (CCA) or depreciation. The CCA rules allow you to write off over a period of years certain large purchases at rates determined by the government. CCA is also a discretionary expense, which means you can defer the claim in the current year or you can claim any amount up to the maximum allowed by the rules.

Since there is so much flexibility with claiming CCA, it is possible to manipulate your income from year to year. This makes using the CCA rules a good personal income-splitting technique. For example, if your income is low one year, you may want to claim less CCA if you expect your income to be at the highest tax level next year. You may get more dollar for your deduction next year, so it may be worth waiting to make the deduction.

However, be warned: with the exception of some fast write-off assets such as computer software and small tools costing less than $500, you cannot double up your deduction. This means that if you choose not to claim CCA one year, the next year you can't claim CCA for both last year and the current year. Each year you can only claim the maximum CCA for that year.

As a general rule, you should claim the maximum CCA you can in the current year. However, if you have lots of loss carry forward or fast write-off assets, you might want to defer claiming CCA in low income years and claim the deduction in high income years to maximize your tax refunds.

> **TAX BEATER**
> Defer claiming CCA on fast write-off assets in low income years to get more dollar for your deduction.

The Corporate Income-Splitting Technique

As the name suggests, corporate income-splitting involves maximizing the lower tax levels of a corporation and your family. It is one of the most sophisticated forms of income-splitting, but also one of the most advantageous.

As of January 1, 2007, Canadian corporations actively involved in a business, like your small or home-based business, can qualify for a very low rate of tax on the first $400,000 of income. (See Round 5 for more details.) In some provinces, this rate can be as low as 13%. By arranging your affairs so that up to $400,000 is taxed within a corporation, you can defer up to 33% in taxes annually. This can mean an annual tax saving of up to $132,000! This could be Round 4's knockout punch.

Eventually, you will want to take this money out of the corporation. What good are tax savings if you can't spend them. When you do, you may pay another tax on the corporation's payment to you. When you add these two taxes together, they will equal approximately what you would have paid if you had received the money directly, without using a corporation.

However, until you need to withdraw that money out of the company, that second level of tax is deferred and you have saved up to $132,000.

TAX BEATER

Use a corporation to smooth income from year-to-year and save tax.

A corporation can also be an effective tool in ensuring that your income personally is smooth from year-to-year, thereby fully utilizing the lower tax levels. As discussed earlier in this round, you can save tax just by ensuring that your income does not fluctuate greatly from year-to-year. With a profitable corporation, you can dictate how much salary you wish to pay yourself and how much earnings to leave behind and have taxed at the corporate level. This provides significant flexibility in planning the remuneration of the owners of the business.

TAX BEATER

Declare bonuses at year-end to defer tax.

In addition, a corporation can be used to defer for a short period of time the tax owing on large profits. The owners of a corporation can declare at any time a bonus to themselves or employees of the business. From the time this bonus is declared, the company has 180 days to pay the bonus and withhold the proper amount of tax. If the owners declare this bonus at the year-end of the corporation, then the bonus will be deductible to the company at the year-end but not taxed to the individual until the bonus is actually paid, 180 days from the year-end. If the company has a July year-end, then the company could get a deduction for the bonus in July and you would not have to report the income until the following year as it would have been paid to you in January. In theory, tax could be deferred on this bonus from say July of 2008 to April 2010 when you have to file your tax return and remit the balance owing. In practice however, there is a requirement to withhold tax on the bonus by the company. The amount of tax required to be withheld is the same as if the bonus was a regular salary being paid out over the course of the year. Accordingly, the opportunity for tax deferral is greatly reduced. However some deferral is available and the corporation certainly provides more planning opportunities.

You can obtain significant tax savings through the use of a corporation, with tax deferral being the name of the game. However, for all but the most successful small and home-based businesses, the use of a corporation is not necessary. For a corporation to be truly useful, your business needs to be earning enough income to maximize your family's personal tax rates and you need to be in a position to leave the savings in the corporation. If you meet these criteria, then consider a corporation.

TAX BEATER
Highly successful small-business entrepreneurs should consider using a corporation to defer up to $116,000 a year in taxes.

Corporate income-splitting can involve the use of several corporations and/or family trusts. Due to the complexities involved with proper corporate income-splitting, I highly recommend you see your tax coach. When your business becomes successful enough to make use of sophisticated corporate income-splitting techniques, it is time to seek proper professional advice. It may seem expensive, but good professional advice will almost always save you money.

To Incorporate or Not?
A Taxing Question

Almost immediately after deciding on what business to start, many entrepreneurs begin thinking about incorporating their businesses. And it's easy to see why. All of the big, successful businesses are corporations. Many of the successful business leaders in your community own and operate businesses that are incorporated. And at cocktail parties everyone is talking about how they own this corporation and that corporation. It makes them appear successful and sophisticated. Owning a corporation can be something of a status symbol. And it's only natural to want to keep up with the Joneses. You're starting a business which you believe will grow and grow and who knows, may become a huge enterprise. But that doesn't mean you should run out now and incorporate. Remember, we want to take every opportunity to "Beat the Taxman." Before we look into whether or not a corporation is right for you, let's first look at what options you have to structure your business.

What Are the Common Business Structures That I Can Use?

The *Income Tax Act* accommodates many complex forms of business structures, most of which would not be looked at by small-business owners or home-based entrepreneurs and are beyond the scope of this book. However, there are three business structures that are common and widely used by small and home-based businesses: sole proprietorship, partnership, and the corporation. Knowing which structure is appropriate for you can save you time and money.

What Is a Sole Proprietorship?

When an individual operates a business and includes the profit or loss of that business on their personal tax return, they are typically considered to be operating as a sole proprietor. There are three characteristics of a sole proprietorship:

1. a single individual owns the business

2. normally the business is in the individual's name or trade name

3. the profits and losses of the business are reported on the individual's personal tax return.

What Are the Advantages of a Sole Proprietorship?

The main advantage of a sole proprietorship has to be the ease of getting started. It can cost little or nothing to start a business as a sole proprietor. And you can start the business immediately. It can be as simple as just starting to keep receipts or opening a bank account. You can register your business name if you wish to use a trade name like "Joe's Garage" or you can just operate as "Joe's," without registering your business name.

A sole proprietorship is by far the easiest structure to set up, which also makes it the most popular with very small and home-based businesses.

Another benefit with this structure is very little government regulation. With a corporation you must operate within the regulations of the *Canada Business Corporations Act* or the provincial equivalent. A partnership is subject to more tax rules and filing requirements than a sole proprietorship.

Overall, the sole proprietorship provides the least government regulation.

The sole proprietor is in control over his or her business and doesn't have to waste time convincing other people that their idea is the right idea.

A last benefit of a sole proprietorship is that all of the profits of the business go to the owner. You won't have to share with anyone the profits of your business. The flip side of this is, of course, that all the losses also go to the owner, which means that you are not sharing the risk of ownership with anyone.

What Are the Disadvantages of a Sole Proprietorship?

The main disadvantage of a sole proprietorship is unlimited liability. Unlimited liability means that you will be personally responsible for all debts and obligations of the business. If your business goes under, you may have to sell personal assets in order to cover the debts of the business.

Another disadvantage of a sole proprietorship is that once the owner passes away or loses interest in the business, the business ceases to operate. With a corporation, the business can live on despite the fact that the owner of the shares retires or dies.

A third disadvantage is that it can often be difficult to raise capital. As a sole proprietor you are the only one responsible for raising money for the business. You don't have partners or investors to help you out financially. However, if you don't need much financing, this isn't much of a concern.

One last disadvantage of being a sole proprietor is the possible perception by fellow business owners that you are unsophisticated. As discussed previously, many people unfortunately think that you must operate a corporation in order to be successful, and to be a good entrepreneur. However, there are many sole proprietors who are very wealthy and sophisticated and there are many owners of corporations who are not wealthy at all and are in no way sophisticated. A business structure does not in itself dictate your level of sophistication. Only time and success will prove that.

What Is a Partnership?

A partnership is best described as two or more sole proprietors who get together to work as a team in one business. A partnership is like a sole proprietorship in that the profit and losses of the partnership are reported on the partners' individual personal tax returns except that, unlike a sole proprietorship, there are two or more owners of the business.

It is important to realize that the ownership of a partnership does not have to be split evenly between the partners. A partnership can be a 50/50 partnership, a 60/40, a 90/5/5 or any other combination, and still qualify as a partnership. A partner typically reports his or her share of the business's profits or losses based on the relative percentage of their ownership in the partnership.

What Are the Advantages of a Partnership?

One of the main advantages of a partnership is ease of formation. Just like a sole proprietorship, a partnership can be formed quite easily and with very little cost. You will have to register the name of a partnership with the province, which is not mandatory for a sole proprietor, but other than that, there are few other registrations required.

Another advantage is the ability to turn to your partners for additional sources of financing for the business. It is no longer simply up to you to borrow money. With a partnership, you have more people providing assistance to help keep the business going.

With a partnership, there are more government regulations than for a sole proprietor, but still far fewer than with a corporation. This will normally reduce the amount you have to pay lawyers and accountants.

A partnership also provides an opportunity to combine the skills of the individual partners. Partnerships often form, for example, because one individual is a fantastic seller and the other individual has the expertise and interest to oversee the making of the product and the administering of the office. Their combined skills produce a more successful team.

And remember, your assets are not the only ones on the line, you get to share the risks of ownership with your partner.

What Are the Disadvantages of a Partnership?

As with a sole proprietorship, unlimited liability is also the main disadvantage of a partnership. You and your partner will be personally liable for all the debts and obligations of your business.

Another problem is divided authority. How do you resolve differences of opinion? You may have to make compromises which are not necessarily good for the business. As well, it may be difficult to find suitable partners. And what if you find someone you think is a suitable partner, only to find out later that they are not up to the task? How do you ask a part owner to leave?

My advice is to have a partnership agreement signed, sealed, and delivered before you start into business. This legal document spells out how the partnership will work. It will ensure that there is a mechanism in place for dealing with differences of opinion, handling the departure or death of one partner, forced resignations, breakup, and major operating issues. Regardless of the number of partners or the size of your business, drawing up a partnership agreement is the right thing to do.

> **TAX BEATER**
> To save money and avoid hassles, develop a partnership agreement.

What Is a Corporation?

A corporation is a separate legal entity. Like a separate person, it must file its own federal and provincial tax returns and register itself with either the provincial or federal government.

As a sole proprietor or a partner, the profits and losses of the business were yours and you reported them on your tax return. As an owner, you don't pay yourself a salary or issue yourself a T4, because you will be reporting your share of the profits on your tax return. But the corporation is a separate entity and, as such, all of the profits and losses are reported on the corporation's federal and provincial tax returns. If you wish to report some corporate income on your own personal tax return, you must pay yourself a wage out of that corporation.

What Are the Advantages of a Corporation?

There are two main advantages of using a corporation. The first addresses the major shortcomings of the other two structures. A corporation can provide limited liability. For the most part, the corporate debts are not an obligation of the individual shareholders.

The other main advantage is income tax savings. It is possible to save considerable tax dollars by using a corporation. However, this is not the case in all circumstances. How you can "Beat the Taxman" with a corporation will be discussed later in this round.

What Are the Disadvantages of a Corporation?

A significant disadvantage of using a corporation is the increased amount of government regulation and the associated costs. If you wish to use a corporation, you must incorporate a company, which can cost you from $300 to $1,500 plus, depending on the complexity of the corporate structure and whether or not you use a lawyer. You will have to complete separate tax returns and financial statements for the corporation resulting in more than doubling the number of tax returns you have to file.

With the added complexity of corporate tax returns, it becomes even more important to solicit the assistance of a tax coach. More tax returns and greater complexity means more professional advice and costs. Under the right circumstances, this is fine. If your business is successful, then the fees you will pay for good advice should outweigh the costs, but the conditions have to be right.

This leads us into the last main disadvantage of a corporation. Sometimes there can actually be a tax cost to using a corporation. With a sole proprietorship or partnership, if your business incurs losses, especially in the start-up years, these losses can be deducted against other sources of income. You can deduct the losses against your pension income, your interest income, or that part-time job you have to pay the bills. If the loss is really substantial, resulting in a taxable loss overall on your tax return, then this loss can be carried back three years and forward twenty, if the loss arose in the 2006 or a later taxation year. If the loss arose between March 22, 2004 and before 2006, it can be carried forward for a period of ten years, and if the loss occurred in a tax year ending before March 22, 2004, then it can be carried forward only seven years to deduct against income in those years. This is a real advantage of sole proprietorships and partnerships.

> **TAX BEATER**
>
> Save taxes in start-up years where you have losses by using the sole proprietorship or partnership structure.

With a corporation, since it is a separate legal entity, the losses cannot be applied against income on your personal tax return. Instead, the losses can only be deducted against income within that corporation. The losses can be carried back three years and forward seven or ten years, but have to remain in the corporation. This is a significant drawback of a corporation when times are tough.

What Tax Savings Can Be Achieved By Using a Corporation?

There are two key objectives in tax planning. The first is to save overall tax dollars; you want to reduce, in absolute terms, the tax that you have to pay. The second and equally important objective is to defer for as long as possible the payment of this tax. By delaying the payment, you, in effect, save money. You now have more money for your business. A corporation is an effective tool in helping with the second objective, deferring the payment of tax dollars.

With a corporation, income is broken down into two main classifications, specified investment income, sometimes referred to as passive income, and active business income. Passive income is income you receive from such things as investments in the stock market, long term GICs, term deposits, bonds, rental income, etc. It is income that is generated automatically, or passively, from an investment.

Active business income is income you receive from business operations. As a small-business entrepreneur, most or all of your business income will be considered active business income. This distinction is important because the Income Tax Act taxes the two types of incomes differently. As of January 1, 2007, the first $400,000 of active business income earned inside a corporation owned by a Canadian resident is taxed at only about 16%. Prior to 2007, only the first $300,000 of active business income earned inside a corporation owned by a Canadian resident was taxed at this low rate. It is important to note that if your corporation has a non-calendar year-end, the $400,000 limit will be prorated. Active business income earned in excess of the $400,000 limit is subject to a federal corporate tax rate of about 22%. On December 17, 2007, legislation was passed to reduce the federal corporate tax rate for active income earned by a corporation to 15% by 2012, starting with a 2.5% reduction for 2008. The federal corporate tax rate will then be reduced by another 0.5 percentage point in 2009, a further 1% in 2010, followed by a 1.5 percentage point reduction in both 2011 and 2012.

Also announced in late 2007 was the federal government's desire to seek collaboration from the provinces and territories to reduce their corporate tax rates in an effort to achieve a combined corporate tax rate of 25% by the year 2012.

In comparison, passive income is taxed at a rate approximately equal to 50% (depending on the province). A portion of the tax is refundable on passive income lowering the tax rate to a more comparable number. However, this refund is only available once a dividend is paid. So until then, active income is taxed around 16% while passive income is taxed around 50%. A significant deferral can be obtained on active business income.

TAX BEATER

Defer up to 28% in taxes by using a corporation properly.

As a small-business entrepreneur, all, or substantially all, of your income will likely be considered active business income and, therefore, will be taxed at the lower rate. The tax deferral works by making use of this lower tax rate inside the corporation. But in order for the tax planning to be really effective, we must also maximize the lower tax rates at the personal level.

Sounds complicated? Well, let's see how it works. Assume for a moment that your company made $200,000. You then pay yourself a salary of $125,000 to maximize the lower tax levels, leaving $75,000 to be taxed in the corporation. At $125,000 in personal income, you are at the top of the Tax Rate Stairway, as discussed in Round 4. Any additional salary paid to you at that level will be taxed at about 46%. If the income is left in the corporation it will be taxed at about 16%. The difference represents a tax deferral of 30%.

TAX DEFERRAL AVAILABLE BY USING A CORPORATION

Assumption: The individual is at the highest tax level.

Alternative 1—Earned Directly by Individual	$
Income Earned by the Individual	75,000
Personal Tax Paid (46%)	(34,500)
Cash in Individual's Hands	40,500
Alternative 2—Earned Through a Corporation	
Income Earned by the Corporation	75,000
Corporate Tax Paid (16%)	(12,000)
Cash Remaining in Corporation	63,000
Tax on Dividend on Distribution of Cash to Shareholder (31%)	(19,530)
Cash in Individual's Hands	43,470
Tax Deferral Available (Tax that can be Delayed on Payment of Dividend)	**19,530**

Note: The $19,530 is not a tax savings but a deferral. The $19,530 tax on the distribution of the dividend is deferred until you actually pay the money out of the corporation, which may not occur for a very long time.

This is only a tax deferral since you haven't yet received that $75,000 out of the corporation. In order to get the $75,000 (less the corporate tax you will pay on the $75,000) out of the corporation, you will need to pay yourself a dividend and pay tax personally on the dividend of about 31%. This rate will vary from province to province and is lower at

TAX BEATER

Distribute corporate retained profits to shareholders when personal income is low.

different levels on the Tax Rate Stairway. The 31% rate being used here is the rate at the highest level on the stairway. However, a common tax planning strategy involves paying these dividends out to the shareholders in either bad years or in retirement when your personal income is lower, resulting in even greater absolute tax savings.

You will notice in the above example that earning your income through the corporation and paying it all out to the owner as a dividend, you have more cash in your pocket. In the example, you have an extra $2,970 cash. This is pretty typical in most provinces that there is an actual tax savings of about 2% by flowing the income through your corporation. While 2% is not a significant tax savings, it does tell us however that there is no downside to using this tax deferral strategy and it does provide a little bonus down the road.

It should be noted that this tax savings only works if you can leave money in the corporation for a number of years. If you need the money for personal reasons and you are constantly removing the cash from the corporation, you will not be able to take advantage of these ideas to "Beat the Taxman."

Is There a Tax Advantage to Selling Shares of My Corporation?

Another significant tax advantage you gain by using a corporation is the ability to use the $500,000 capital gains exemption on the sale of the shares (if they are disposed of before March 19, 2007). In December 2007, legislation was passed to increase the capital gains exemption by $250,000 to $750,000 for dispositions that occur on or after March 19, 2007. The capital gains exemption received a considerable amount of press and discussion in 1994 and 1995 when the federal government announced in the February 22, 1994 budget the elimination of the $100,000 capital gains exemption. The $100,000 capital gains exemption was available on other property like shares listed on the stock market, mutual funds, and cottage property. (The use of the capital gains exemption on cottage property really ended in 1992.)

But what didn't receive as much press at the time was that the capital gains exemption can still be used on the sale of shares in a qualified small Canadian-owned business or qualified farm property. And that this capital gains exemption is $750,000 in value for dispositions occurring on or after March 19, 2007. Talk about "Beating the Taxman." This one idea could save you approximately $172,500 in income taxes. The capital gains exemption is now also available on the transfer of certain fishing properties disposed of on or after May 2, 2006.

> **TAX BEATER**
>
> Save thousands of dollars by selling shares that qualify for the $500,000 capital gains exemption.

With this in mind, there can be a significant advantage to selling shares of your business rather than selling assets. How-ever, it is often difficult to find a buyer who is willing to purchase shares. There are risks associated with buying someone else's shares and a tax incentive for the buyer to purchase assets. So if you want to sell shares, you will normally have to discount the price, which will start to reduce your tax benefits. And depending on your personal tax returns, you may not be able to make use of the capital gains exemption. The government restricts the use of this exemption in some cases where taxpayers have claimed investment losses.

If you can make use of the exemption and you can structure the deal to be a sale of shares, you can save considerable tax dollars. Be aware however, that this is an extremely complex area of tax legislation. If you're planning to sell your business in the near future, I strongly advise you to seek out a good tax coach to have in your corner. If done incorrectly, the sale of shares could cost you more than if you had just sold assets in a straightforward deal.

Should I Take Advantage of the Capital Gains Exemption Now?

The $750,000 capital gains exemption on shares in a qualified small business corporation or qualified farm and fishing property is an exceptional tax savings tool. With the elimination of the $100,000 capital gains exemption, many taxpayers have worried that the government will take away the $750,000 exemption as well and have performed what is called a crystallization of their capital gains exemption. Many others continue to contemplate whether or not a crystallization is for them. The following comments relate to using the capital gains exemption now for shares in a qualified small business corporation. If you are considering using the capital gains exemption on qualified farm property, my advice would be to seek out the advice of a professional tax coach that is familiar with farm tax rules. There are a number of very specific and individual issues that should be addressed before deciding if this planning is appropriate for you.

A crystallization on shares of a qualified small business corporation effectively invokes the capital gains exemption and adds the amount of the exemption that you have used to the cost of your shares in the company. Later, if you sell your shares to a stranger, the increased cost base of your shares will significantly reduce your tax liability.

Another reason some taxpayers have crystallized their capital gains exemption is for estate planning purposes. In order to be able to use the capital gains exemption, the corporation must meet the very stringent definition of a *Qualified Small Business Corporation* (QSBC). One of the keys to this definition is that at least 90% of the assets of the corporation are actively used in the business at the time of using the capital gains exemption. So if you have excess cash sitting around in the company, you could be offside with this rule and not qualify for the capital gains exemption.

TAX BEATER

Crystallize your capital gains exemption on QSBC shares to ensure its tax benefits for the future.

Under normal circumstances, when you are planning to make use of the exemption, you can easily ensure that all excess cash and investments are removed from the company. However, if there was a sudden and untimely death of the shareholder of the company, then you can't plan for the removal of excess cash and investments and the deceased executor might not be able to make use of the exemption. Accordingly, it is sometimes wise to make use of the exemption now to ensure its tax benefits in the future.

You should be careful if you are planning to make use of this exemption, however. As discussed earlier, there could be some tax consequences of crystallizing your capital gains exemption. If you have previously claimed business investment losses on your tax return or have reported a greater amount of investment expenses than investment income since 1988, then you could be faced with a tax cost on using the exemption. Additionally, if you wish to deduct business investment losses in the future, you will be limited by the amount of the exemption you have claimed in the past.

So, in determining whether or not you should crystallize your capital gains exemption, consider the advantages and make sure there are no serious adverse tax consequences to the procedure. If you don't, you may end up the loser on this strategy.

Can I Increase the Capital Gains Exemption?

While the amount of the capital gains exemption is limited to $750,000, it should be remembered that everyone has this lifetime limit of $750,000. If you are the only shareholder in your company, then you will be the only person eligible for making use of the exemption. However, if both you and your spouse own shares in the company, then both you and your spouse would be eligible to make use of the $750,000 capital gains exemption on a sale of shares to an individual or an non-family owned corporation. This works out to sheltering up to $1.5 million from tax. Now if you happen to have two children that also own shares in the company, then they each would have a $750,000 capital gains exemption and you could potentially shelter $3 million from tax.

By increasing the number of shareholders in a company, you also increase the amount of the capital gains exemption that could ultimately be used. If you plan to get your family involved, however, make sure they pay fair value for the shares they purchase or else this planning could be null and void. Additionally, they will need to own the shares for at least two years prior to any sale, so plan this one early.

TAX BEATER

Include your family as shareholders and increase the tax savings on a sale.

Can I Take Advantage of the New Enhanced Dividend Rules?

As of February 21, 2007, the tax planning opportunities for both small and large corporations became even more complex. This is because, on February 21, 2007, legislation was passed on how the new rules for the taxation of dividends will work. The purpose of these new rules is to try to level the tax playing field between the taxation of income through a Canadian public company through to the individual shareholder as compared to the taxation of Income Trusts. If the provinces fully come on side (you should consult with your tax coach to determine your province's position) then the total tax paid by investors in Income Trusts and Canadian public companies will be almost identical.

The taxation of public companies and income trusts are beyond the scope of this book. However, these new rules also apply to the small Canadian Controlled Private Company and, therefore, may in fact be applicable to your company. But I warn you, the new rules are complicated and the advice of a good tax coach would benefit you well in this area of tax planning.

How Do the New Dividend Rules Work?

The idea behind these new rules is that certain corporations will be able to pay dividends (let's call these eligible dividends) to their shareholders and these eligible dividends will be taxed at a better rate, as compared to non-eligible or regular dividends. Only income taxed at the high general corporate tax rate can be paid out as an eligible dividend. So to track this, the government has proposed that a company's income should be categorized into two different pools. One pool is called the "General Rate Income Pool" and the other is the "Low Rate Income Pool."

The "General Rate Income Pool" (GRIP) will keep track of all of the corporation's profits that were taxed at the high rate of tax. This means that any profits that were taxed at the lower small business rate of tax or profits that were subject to any manufacturing and processing credits will not be part of this pool. Additionally, investment income or passive income that is eligible for the refundable tax will not form part of the pool.

The "Low Rate Income Pool" (LRIP) will keep track of all of the corporation's profits that were taxed at a more preferential rate of tax, including those taxed at the small business rate. This means that if your corporation claims the small business deduction, the after-tax profits will be added to this pool.

To start, dividends are paid out of a corporation's after-tax earnings, and are then taxed in the hands of the recipient. Therefore, tax is essentially being paid twice, first by the corporation, and again by the recipient. However, as shown in alternative 2 of the tax deferral chart on page 69, if the corporate tax rate is low, as in the case of income taxed at the small business rate, the combined corporate tax and the personal tax on the bonus is close to or less than the tax that would be paid on that income if paid directly to the individual. This is called corporate integration and it works for the most part with businesses eligible for the low small business tax rate.

If, however, you increase the corporate tax rate to the general tax rate of say 33%, which is what a public company might pay or a company not eligible for the small business deduction, then the corporate integration breaks down. For example, assume a company that is not eligible for the small business deduction makes $1,000 of income and has to decide if it should pay the income out to the owner as a bonus or have it taxed through the company and paid to the owner as a dividend. The following chart shows that by paying the $1,000 through the company, extra tax of $80 is paid as compared to paying a salary. This represents an overall tax rate of approximately 54%, as compared to the highest personal tax rate of about 46%.

Alternative 1 – Earned Directly by Individual	**$**
Income Earned by the Individual	1,000
Personal Tax Paid (46%)	(460)
Cash in Individual's Hands	540

Alternative 2 – Earned Through a Corporation

Income Earned by the Corporation	1,000
Corporate Tax Paid (33%)	(330)
Cash Remaining in Corporation	670
Tax on Dividend on Distribution of Cash to Shareholder (31%)	(210)
Cash in Individual's Hands	460
Total Additional Tax Paid in Alternative 2	**80**

The new enhanced dividend tax rules attempt to provide better corporate integration with companies that do not benefit from the low small business tax rate. The new rules accomplish this by providing a tax break to the individual on the dividends received from income taxed at the general income tax rate or from the GRIP pool. As can be seen in the following chart, the tax now paid by the individual on the dividend is only $130. This reduces the overall tax paid by flowing income through the corporation to be close, if not equal, to the tax paid at the personal level.

Alternative 1 – Earned Directly by Individual	**$**
Income Earned by the Individual	1,000
Personal Tax Paid (46%)	(460)
Cash in Individual's Hands	540

Alternative 2 – Earned Through a Corporation	
Income Earned by the Corporation	1,000
Corporate Tax Paid (33%)	(330)
Cash Remaining in Corporation	670
Tax on Dividend on Distribution of Cash to Shareholder (20%)	(130)
Cash in Individual's Hands	540
Total Additional Tax Paid in Alternative 2	**0**

How Do the New Dividend Rules Impact My Business?

If you are a shareholder of a Canadian Controlled Private Corporation you will now be faced with the decision of whether your company will claim the small business deduction and declare a bonus for any income in excess of the amount eligible for the lower tax rates, or have the income taxed at the higher rates and declare an eligible dividend.

The decision of whether to bonus down to the small business limit or declare an eligible dividend is a very complicated one, one that you will need to discuss with your tax coach. There are a number of issues surrounding the decision that will require careful consideration and analysis. For example, some provincial governments have announced that they will phase-in the provincial side of these new dividend rules over a period of two to four years, in which case it may take some time before you realize the full benefit of new tax legislation. Also, some provincial governments impose a claw-back of the small business deduction by imposing a surtax for income over the provincial small business limit.

You should also note that the proposed new rules allow companies to go back to 2001 and include any income that was taxed at the general tax rate into their opening General Rate Income Pool. Therefore, a careful review of past years may be in order to make sure you can take full advantage of these new rules.

Needless to say, the rules surrounding the new dividend rules are very complex, and making the mistake of declaring an eligible dividend out of ineligible profits can be costly. The penalty for making this mistake is a tax of 20% of the dividend! That's one punch you definitely want to protect yourself against! Again, the importance of finding yourself a good tax coach and discussing this with them cannot be understated!

So Which Structure Is Best for Me?

Determining which structure is best for you is one of the more difficult decisions you will have to make. Once again the advice of a tax coach can be invaluable.

But in the meantime, here is a good rule of thumb. If you need all the profit that the business is generating to cover living expenses, a corporation is likely not for you. Remember, one of the main advantages of the corporate structure is the ability to defer income by leaving profit in the corporation. If you need all the money generated by your business for personal needs, you won't be able to take advantage of the tax deferral.

The other key advantage to a corporation may be to protect your personal assets in the event of an unforeseen business loss. Earlier, we discussed the concept of limited liability. This means that a corporation's unsecured creditors can take no action against the personal assets of the owner in the event that the corporation does not pay its creditors. Unfortunately, banks and trust companies and many trade suppliers won't loan new corporations money without excellent security and, in most cases, that security can include the owner's personal guarantee. When this happens, the corporation does not protect the owner's personal assets.

However, if you operate a business where the risk of accident or lawsuit is high, for example, a small construction company, a corporation may be useful in providing you additional protection. Generally, you would insure against accidents or lawsuits; however, if the losses from these actions exceeded your insurance coverage, then the corporation would act as a shield in protecting your remaining personal assets.

But if it is unlikely that you are going to be sued for large amounts, if you don't have significant unsecured creditors, and if you are not taking advantage of any of our tax deferral ideas, then more likely a corporation is not for you.

TAX BEATER

Save taxes by transferring profitable businesses into a corporation and keeping losing businesses as sole proprietorships.

Here's one last thing to think about when trying to decide whether or not you should use a corporation. It is possible to transfer all or any part of a business operating as a sole proprietorship or a partnership into a corporation at any time, tax free. So the best advice usually is to operate as a sole proprietorship or a partnership until your business is established and you can determine if a corporation will be of benefit to you. If you decide that a corporation will provide some tax benefits, roll the business tax free into the corporation at that time. Often the worst tax planning is to start up a business in a corporation that is losing money and you have no way of deducting those losses against personal income. It is better to keep the business outside the corporation until it starts becoming profitable and then transfer it to the corporation.

GST:
Friend or Foe?

Despite what some might say, the GST is here to stay. Governments may change the name of the tax, or get other provinces involved, but some form of consumption tax, like the GST, is going to remain a part of our tax structure for some time to come. You just can't replace the revenues that the GST is providing without creating a new tax or increasing the current tax rates. Both alternatives would mean political suicide in the current environment. So, like it or not, the GST is here to stay.

So if the GST is going to stick around for awhile, maybe it's time you look carefully at your business to ensure that you are minimizing the GST you pay on a year-to-year basis. This round will review in general terms how the GST works, but more importantly, it will highlight what you should know to minimize the GST you pay.

What Is an Input Tax Credit?

An input tax credit is the term used for providing a refund to a business for the GST it pays on its purchases. All businesses

that are selling taxable goods and services, and who are registered, are eligible for a refund of the GST that they pay on
their purchases. What this means is that for most businesses,
the GST is not a tax to them at all. On the one hand, a business
charges and collects for the government the GST on its sales.
On the other hand, the business will pay GST on its purchases,
but the government refunds to the business the GST on these
purchases. There is no tax cost to the business from being registered for the GST.

There can, however, be administrative costs associated
with keeping track of the GST. The "hassle factor" on the
GST can be fairly high. As well, there can be a cost associated
with "cash-flowing" the GST, as the government will want
their money even if you haven't collected your money from
the customer. This makes us ask the question: "is the GST
our friend or our foe?" The GST is friendlier to businesses
than income taxes and payroll taxes, as it is not a direct cost
of doing business. Yet the GST is our enemy when we make
those personal purchases which are not eligible for any input
tax credit rebate. Friend or foe, it's up to you to decide.

Do I Have to Register for the GST?

You must register for the GST if your sales of taxable goods
and services during the fiscal period of your business exceed
$30,000. You are required to register and begin charging the
GST the month after you reach the $30,000 threshold. You
cannot wait until the following year to register.

Up until January 1, 2008 most goods and services sold in
Canada are taxed at the 6% federal GST rate. In the fall of
2007, the federal government announced that it would be decreasing the GST/HST by 1 percentage point to 5%. This
decrease in the rate of GST was effective January 1, 2008.
Some goods and services however, are taxed at a 0% rate. I
recognize that a 0% tax rate appears unusual. You might ask
why not just call these goods and services non-taxable goods
and services? Well, the distinction of non-taxable goods and
services and goods and services taxed at 0% is important.

In order to be eligible to claim a refund of GST on your purchases, you must be selling taxable goods and services. Goods and services subject to a tax rate of 0% would still qualify the business for a refund of GST on its purchases since the sales are taxable. Companies that sell goods and services that are non-taxable or exempt from tax are not eligible for a refund of GST on their purchases. This is a very important distinction indeed. Examples of goods and services subject to the 0% tax rate, or what is referred to as zero-rated goods and services, are listed below.

> **TAX BEATER**
> Register for GST if you are selling zero-rated goods and services to obtain refund of GST on purchases.

EXAMPLES OF ZERO-RATED GOODS AND SERVICES

- sales of basic groceries (e.g., milk, bread, and vegetables)

- sales of agricultural products, farm livestock, and most fishery products

- sales of prescription drugs and drug dispensing fees

- sales of medical devices (e.g., hearing aids and artificial teeth)

- all exports (goods and services taxable in Canada are zero-rated if exported)

Source: Canada Revenue Agency

If you sell what is referred to as *exempt goods and services*, you will not be required to register at all. Registration is not required since you cannot charge GST on your sales, nor are you eligible to receive a refund of GST on your purchases. GST will, under these circumstances, become a real tax cost to your business. Examples of exempt goods and services that might be common among small business and home-based entrepreneurs are listed on the following page.

EXAMPLES OF EXEMPT GOODS AND SERVICES

- sales of used residential housing

- residential rents of one month or more and residential condominium fees

- most health, medical, and dental services performed by licensed physicians or dentists
- child-care services provided primarily to children 14 years old and younger
- legal aid services
- music lessons
- arranging for and issuing insurance policies by insurance companies, agents, and brokers

Source: Canada Revenue Agency

Should I Register for the GST?

If you are not required to register for the GST, and you sell taxable goods and services, you will be left with the question of whether you should register for the GST voluntarily. This is a difficult question, one that can only be answered by looking at each individual's personal situation. Before you make your decision, here are some issues to think about.

First of all, as a registrant you will be eligible for input tax credits. This means that by registering you will be able to reduce the cost of your purchases subject to GST by 5%. This is a significant reduction in the cost of your operations.

TAX BEATER

Register for the GST and increase profits.

Secondly, you will have to start charging GST on sales to your customers. How will this affect you from a competitive point of view? If none of your competitors are charging GST, then maybe you will lose customers if you become registered and start charging GST. If all your competitors are charging GST, registering may allow you to be more competitive, passing on your GST savings to your customers.

Additionally, you need to look at who your major customers are. If most of your customers are businesses that would also be registered for the GST, then they won't care if you're registered or not. The GST won't be a cost to them. And as I noted, since registering reduces your costs, you increase your profits or decrease your prices.

Remember one firm rule: once your taxable sales exceed $30,000 in a taxation year, you are required to register for GST in the following month.

One last factor is that input tax credits on supplies and services used in your business can only be claimed from the date of registration. For example, if you operate your business for a year without being registered, you won't be able to go back and claim an input tax credit on the GST you paid on the stationary you used, or on the legal services you received. Since you were not registered at the time, you are not eligible for the input tax credit. This is one reason why many new small-business entrepreneurs register for the GST immediately.

> **TAX BEATER**
>
> Register for the GST at start up and claim input tax credits on all your business purchases.

How Does the Decrease in the Rate of GST Affect My Business?

As I mentioned earlier, effective January 1, 2008 the rates for the GST and HST were reduced by 1% to 5% and 13%, respectively. What this means for your business is that you will now need to be aware of the timing of your sales made on and around January 1, 2008. Generally:

- If you make a sale, and the GST or HST becomes payable or was paid in 2007, the old GST rate of 6% or HST rate of 14% applies.

- If you make a sale, and the GST or HST becomes payable on or after January 1, 2008, or was paid on or after January 1, 2008, then the rate of 5% GST or 13% HST will apply.

Can I Simplify the Administration of the GST?

One of the major disadvantages of the GST for businesses is having to keep track of all the GST that you pay and collect.

Recording GST in journals can increase significantly the amount of time spent on record-keeping. However, for small businesses there are solutions; in fact, there are two solutions.

In recognizing that recording the GST is a hassle, the government decided to offer two simplified methods to assist in the reporting of the GST for small businesses. The two methods are called the "Simplified Method," used to calculate input tax credits, and the "Quick Method," used to calculate your net GST remittance.

Simplified Method

With the "Simplified Method" you do not have to record separately in your books the GST on your purchases. Normally, if you wish to claim an input tax credit, you would have to go through and add up all of the GST you paid on all of your purchases during the period. If you are keeping a journal, you would keep a separate column reserved for the GST and record in that column the GST that you paid. With the "Simplified Method," you are not required to do this calculation.

Instead, what you would do is simply add up all of your taxable purchases and multiply this number by 5/105 (13/113 for HST purchases, see page 103). For example, if all of your taxable supplies, including the GST and other non-refundable provincial and other taxes total $2,000, you would be eligible for an input tax credit of $92.24 ($2,000 x 5/105). This method can save time and money.

In order to qualify for the simplified method, taxable sales and taxable purchases in the preceding year can not have exceeded $500,000 and $2 million respectively. If you qualify, just start using this method at the beginning of your fiscal year. If you start using this method, you must stay with it for at least one year, unless you no longer qualify.

The problem with the simplified method is that it still requires you to separate taxable purchases from non-taxable purchases. For example, employee salaries, insurance, interest on loans, and other exempt or zero-rated purchases must be separated from the taxable purchases so you can calculate the input tax credit. For some businesses this is not a problem, and due to the volume of taxable purchases, real savings can be achieved. With other businesses, because they make few purchases, it may be just as easy to separate out the GST. If this method can save you time, consider using it.

Quick Method

If the "Simplified Method" didn't seem easy enough, maybe the "Quick Method" will be more to your liking. The "Quick Method" is truly a simple way to calculate and remit GST. If you can qualify to use this method, all you need to do is collect the GST on your taxable sales and then remit to the government 1.8%, or 4.4% of the total sales including GST (4.4% or 8.8% for businesses located in a participating province and selling within a participating province, see page 104). With this method, you do not calculate or obtain input tax credits on normal business expenses. These input tax credits are replaced with the portion of the 5% sales tax not remitted to the GST office.

For example, if during the past year you had taxable sales of $100,000 including GST, and you qualified for the 4.4% rate, (see explanation later in this section) then you would have collected $4,762 from your customers (calculated as $100,000 x 5/105). Of this $4,762 that you have collected from your customers, you remit to the government $4,400 ($100,000 x 4.4%). This leaves you with $362 as your input tax credit. If the actual GST paid for the year for which you are eligible for an input tax credit was less than $362 then you will be better off using the "Quick Method."

TAX BEATER
Reduce tax and simplify GST record-keeping by using the "Quick Method."

If your actual input tax credits would have been greater than the $362 in this case, then you will have to weigh the cost of losing eligible input tax credits against the additional time and aggravation of calculating the input tax credit.

To be eligible to use this method, your annual taxable sales including GST must be less than $200,000. In addition, there are a number of industries that will not qualify under the program (see below). To start using the "Quick Method," complete GST form 74, "Election and Revocation Form for the Quick Method of Accounting" and send it your local CRA district taxation office.

TYPES OF BUSINESSES NOT ELIGIBLE TO USE "QUICK METHOD"

- accounting
- audit services
- financial consulting
- lawyer or law offices
- insurance
- dealer in financial instruments
- notary public
- tax preparation services
- tax consulting

Source: Canada Revenue Agency

TAX BEATER

Maximize your GST savings by claiming the 1% reduction.

TAX BEATER

Remember to claim input tax credits on capital purchases when using the "Quick Method."

The 3.6% "Quick Method" rate applies to service businesses. Examples might include dry cleaners, consulting businesses, delivery businesses, etc. The 1.8% "Quick Method" rate is reserved for retailers and wholesalers. Typically with these types of businesses there is a higher rate of taxable purchases. Accordingly, the "Quick Method" rate is lower. If you are unsure which rate to use, your local district taxation office can help you.

If you elect to use the "Quick Method," keep in mind the 1% reduction in both rates on your first $30,000 of sales. As an incentive to use this method, for the first $30,000 of sales the rates are only 3.6% and 0.8%. Once your sales, including GST, go over the $30,000 mark, you must start remitting based on 3.6% or 1.8% as appropriate in your case.

If you are using the "Quick Method," make sure you still claim input tax credits on your capital purchases like computers, office equipment, machinery, vehicles, and even software. The "Quick Method" is meant to reduce the administrative burden on everyday business sales and purchases. With the not-so-everyday purchases of vehicles and equipment, you are still eligible to claim an input tax credit. When you sell used capital goods like old computers, your vehicle, etc., then you will also have to remit the GST on the sale, over and above the "Quick Method" calculation.

TAX BEATER
Claim forgotten input tax credits before the four-year limitation is up.

Can I Still Claim Input Tax Credits If I Forgot to File My GST Return?

If you have registered for the GST, you have up to four years from the day the GST return was due for the period in which the purchase was made to claim your input tax credit on the purchase, provided your taxable sales were less than $6 million and you were not a listed financial institution. For example, assume you must file your GST returns quarterly, and you make a purchase of a $20,000 vehicle, used exclusively in your business, in January, 2003. The GST you paid on the vehicle is $1,400. The year-end of your business is December 31, 2005. You will have until April 30, 2009, to claim that input tax credit.

With a December year-end, the first quarter of 2005 ends in March. Your GST return is due one month after the end of the quarter. You then have up to four years from that date to claim any forgotten input tax credits. After the four years, you won't be able to apply for the refund.

Can I Be Denied a Legitimate Input Tax Credit?

To claim an input tax credit, you must have invoices or receipts containing certain information. The amount of information varies depending on the invoice amount. The table on the next page shows what information is required for different invoice amounts.

**INFORMATION IS REQUIRED FOR DIFFERENT
INVOICE AMOUNTS**

Information Required	Total Purchase Under $30	Total Purchase $30 to $149.99	Total Purchase $150 or more
Your business or trading name	✔	✔	✔
The date of the invoice	✔	✔	✔
The total amount paid or payable	✔	✔	✔
Detail on what is subject to GST and either the total amount of GST charged or a note that the total includes GST		✔	✔
Your GST registration number		✔	✔
The purchaser's name or trading name			✔
Terms of payment			✔
A brief description of the goods or services			✔

Source: Canada Revenue Agency

TAX BEATER

Request GST information be included on purchase invoices to save money and hassles.

If a receipt or invoice for a purchase you make does not contain the proper information, the government can deny the input tax credit on the purchase. The key detail that Canada Revenue Agency auditors look for in most cases is the GST registration number. If the purchase is for more than $30 and there is no GST registration number on the purchase invoice or sales receipt, the tax auditor may deny your input tax credit.

The onus is on you, the purchaser who is claiming an input tax credit, to ensure that all the information is present to substantiate your claim. If you are being charged GST and the invoice you are receiving does not provide the required information, ask for it to be written on the invoice. It could save you hassles and money later on.

How Can I Verify That One of My Suppliers Is Registered for GST/HST?

As I mentioned previously, the onus is on you to ensure that the invoice you are paying, and claiming an ITC for, qualifies for the tax credit. This includes the situation of a supplier providing you with a false GST number on their invoice. The Canada Revenue Agency has taken the position that it is up to you to verify that your supplier is properly registered for GST and, therefore, your ITC claim is valid. Even if the invoice looks correct with what appears to be a proper GST number, if the number is false then your ITC claim will be denied.

To assist taxpayers in determining if a supplier is registered for GST/HST, the CRA has created an internet-based GST/HST registry website. With this registry you can verify whether or not one of your suppliers is registered to collect GST/HST. The registry's website is http://www.cra-arc.gc.ca/eservices/tax/business/gsthstregistry. In order to use the registry you will require three pieces of information:

1. The first 9 digits of a business' GST number;

2. The business' name as registered with the Canada Revenue Agency; and

3. The date of the transaction in question.

Given that the web-based registry now provides businesses with the ability to confirm whether a particular business is registered for GST or whether a particular registration number belongs to a supplier, the courts are likely to be less lenient in allowing ITC claims when the supporting documentation does not include a registration number belonging to that particular vendor. For this reason I would recommend maintaining copies of the GST/HST registration confirmation of any new suppliers in case your ITC claim is ever questioned. If you find that you are trying to use the registry and you are unable to obtain confirmation that a business is registered for GST, as may be the case where you do not have the company's registered name, then I would recommend calling the CRA to obtain the status of a company's GST registration.

Can I Claim an Input Tax Credit on Capital Purchases?

One of the most often forgotten claims for input tax credits relates to the GST paid on capital purchases. This happens because capital purchases are not recorded the same way as normal everyday expenses. It's not every day that you go out and buy a computer. So when you record the computer in your books, you may forget about the GST you paid. Or when you add up the GST you paid from all your regular, day-to-day invoices, you may forget about that special purchase of the computer.

Sometimes, the GST paid on a capital purchase is so large in comparison to your normal activity that it will result in a GST refund when you file your GST return. Many times, taxpayers believe that there must be some kind of mistake! The government is paying them money! After all these years of paying the government GST when they file their tax returns, they're amazed.

But it is possible, and happens very frequently, that the government will pay the taxpayer instead of the other way around. And refunding the GST on capital purchases is one of the common reasons for this occurrence.

GST on capital purchases is refundable as long as the capital item is being used for business purposes. So don't forget to include it as an input tax credit and get back the GST you deserve.

TAX BEATER

Remember to include input tax credits on capital purchases used in your business.

Can I Claim an Input Tax Credit on an Asset Purchased Before I Registered for the GST?

You have been operating your business, buying assets like computers, fax machines, office furniture and you haven't registered for the GST because your sales weren't that great. Now you decide you should or have to register, can you claim an input tax credit for all these assets you purchased before

TAX BEATER

Claim ITCs on assets purchased prior to registering for the GST and still being used in the business.

you registered? The answer, yes. You can't claim an input tax credit on purchases consumed in your business prior to registering, but you can on assets that you are still using in your business. And you have four years from the time of filing that first GST return to claim the input tax credit.

The amount of an input tax credit you can claim is calculated on an asset by asset basis. It is equal to the lesser of:

a) the GST actually paid on the asset for which you have not yet received an input tax credit, and

b) the amount of GST you would pay on that particular asset if you were to have purchased it from a stranger at the time you registered for the GST.

You can also claim an input tax credit on services that became payable before you registered for the GST if the services were provided after you registered for the GST. Additionally, you can claim an input tax credit on rent you paid before you registered that was for a period of time after you became a registrant. The idea is that you can claim an input tax credit on the GST you paid for any goods or services that you will be using after you register.

> **TAX BEATER**
>
> Claim ITCs on services that were paid prior to registering but were used after registering.

Can I Claim Input Tax Credits on Personal Capital Property?

You can generally claim a full input tax credit on personal capital property as long as you use the property in your business for more than 50% of the time and your business sales are subject to GST. Personal capital property refers to most types of capital assets like computers, office equipment, and office furniture. Personal capital property does not include real property like land and buildings and small capital purchases like software and small tools costing less than $200 (if purchased before May 2, 2006) or $500 if acquired after May 2, 2006.

For example, if you purchased a computer which you use 75% of the time in your business and 25% of the time personally, you would be eligible to claim an input tax credit of 100%

> **TAX BEATER**
>
> Claim Input Tax Credits on personal capital property used more than 50% of the time in your taxable business.

of the GST paid (provided that your business was registered for GST and sold only taxable goods and services). On the other hand, if you purchased some furniture which is used 45% of the time for business purposes, and 55% of the time for personal purposes, you would not be eligible to claim any input tax credit for the GST you paid.

For real property like land and buildings, the rules are a little more complicated. If you operate your business as a sole proprietor and you use the property you purchased more than 50% of the time for personal use, then you are not eligible for any input tax credit. If you use the property for commercial purposes between 50% and 90% of the time then you may claim a prorated ITC based on your percentage business use. If you use the property more than 90% of the time for business purposes you can claim 100% ITC on the purchase of the property. If you operate your business as a partnership or corporation the rules change slightly, in that if you use the property 10% or less for business purposes you are not entitled to any ITC, and if you use the property more than 90% of the time for business purposes you are entitled to 100% ITC refund. In all other cases you prorate your ITC based on your percentage business usage.

Can I Claim Input Tax Credits on Personal Vehicles?

Personal passenger vehicles used in your business are considered capital assets, however, they are not subject to the same general rules as described above. If your personal vehicle is used in your business, you will generally be eligible to claim an input tax credit on the vehicle, however, the rules for how much you can claim are unfortunately overly complex. These rules also apply to personal aircraft used in your business.

The first thing to be aware of is that these rules apply to sole proprietors and partnerships using personal vehicles in a business. When you use your personal vehicle in your business and it is used 90% of the time or more for business purposes then you can claim 100% of the input tax credit paid. If the vehicle is a passenger vehicle (see Round 10) than the maximum you can claim is $1,500 (5% of $30,000). If the vehicle is not a passenger vehicle than you can claim the amount of GST paid.

When the vehicle is used less than 90% of the time in the business, you can only claim as an input tax credit, 5/105ths of the capital cost allowance (CCA) claimed in the year. CCA is the amount of depreciation that you are allowed to claim on capital assets in the year. How much CCA you can claim on a passenger vehicle is discussed in more detail in Round 10. The amount you claim as an input tax credit in a year must then be subtracted from the CCA pool in the next year.

I warned you this was overly complex. Maybe an example will help. Say you purchase a vehicle costing $20,000 including 5% GST which you use 60% of the time in your business. In the first year, the maximum CCA you can claim is $1,800 ($20,000 cost x 30% CCA rate x 1/2 rate for first year x 60% business use). The amount of the input tax credit that you can claim is $1,800 x 5/105 or $86. In the next year you subtract from the original cost of the vehicle, the CCA you claimed this year and the ITC that you claimed. Therefore, for year 2 your maximum CCA claim would be $3,260 ($20,000 cost − $1,800 first year's CCA − $86 first year's ITC x 30% CCA rate x 60% business use). Your input tax credit claim for the second year would be $155 ($3,260 CCA x 5/105).

If the business use of your passenger vehicle is 10% or less, then you will not be eligible for any input tax credit.

If your business is incorporated then you can generally claim full input tax credits provided that the vehicle is used more than 50% of the time for eligible business purposes subject to the passenger vehicle restrictions as discussed above and in Round 10. If the vehicle is used 50% or less of the time for eligible business purposes, then no input tax credit can be claimed.

Can I Claim Full Input Tax Credits on All General Business Expenses?

There are limitations to the amount of input tax credits you can claim on your business's operating expenses. General operating expenses are all the normal expenses that you incur on a day-to-day basis and might include office supplies, utilities, and repairs and maintenance.

If general operating expenses are used in your business 90% of the time or more and all of your business sales are subject to GST, then you will be able to claim 100% of the input tax credit on the GST you paid.

On the other hand, if the business use of an operating expense is 10% or less, then you will not be able to claim *any* input tax credit on the GST you paid. Anywhere in between and you will be able to claim only a portion of the input tax credit.

For example, assume that your business involves the developing of web sites for the Internet. You are registered for GST and all of your sales are taxable. Assume that you purchased some blank computer diskettes for your business. If you expect that the diskettes will be used 90% of the time or greater in your web site design business, then you would be able to deduct 100% of the GST on those diskettes.

On the other hand, if the diskettes might be used only 60% of the time for your business and the other 40% of the time they are used to store computer games and personal items, then you would be eligible to claim only 60% of the input tax credits.

If you purchase the diskettes and they are rarely used in the business, you would not be able to claim any input tax credit for the GST you paid on their purchase.

There is also a limitation on claiming input tax credits if you are engaged in another business activity that sells exempt goods and services. You must prorate the GST on a reasonable basis between the two businesses and then claim an input tax credit on the taxable business.

TAX BEATER

Claim Input Tax Credits on general operating expenses for items used more than 10% of the time in a taxable business.

For example, assume that you have the web site design business but you also have a business selling life insurance. The selling of life insurance is an exempt business; therefore, purchases relating to that business would not qualify for an input tax credit. Say you purchased the computer diskettes for both the web site design business and the life insurance business and the allocation between the two businesses is 60% and 40% respectively. You would therefore be allowed to claim an input tax credit of 60% on the GST paid because 60% of the purchase related to the taxable web site design business.

Are There Any Other Restrictions on Claiming Input Tax Credits?

There are many restrictions on claiming input tax credits. This is one reason the legislation is so complex. Many of the restrictions would not involve the typical small-business entrepreneur. However, there are a few which would be common among many small-business owners.

The first such restriction relates to meals and entertainment expenses. For general income tax purposes you are eligible to claim only 50% of meals and entertainment expenses as a business deduction. The GST legislation mirrors the income tax legislation in this area by allowing you to claim an input tax credit of only 50% of the GST paid on meals and entertainment.

Another restriction relates to the GST paid on membership fees or dues paid to any recreational, dining, or sporting facility. For example, the GST paid on your golf membership, the fitness club membership, or your dues at the hunting and fishing club would not be eligible for an input tax credit. Even if there is a legitimate business reason for having the membership, the GST would not be eligible for the tax credit, just as the membership would not be deductible as a business expense under the *Income Tax Act* (see Round 7). The one exception might be if you purchase memberships and then resell them as part of your business.

When Do I Have to File My GST Return?

When you register for the GST, Canada Revenue Agency will assign you a reporting period based on your anticipated level of sales. As your sales levels fluctuate, your reporting requirements may also fluctuate. If you have taxable sales of less than $6,000,000 annually, you will have an option of how you want to file your GST return. If your sales are greater than $6,000,000, there is no option, you must file your GST return monthly.

In an effort to reduce the amount of paperwork associated with filing tax forms and remitting taxes, the 2007 federal budget proposed to reduce the frequency of such filings for small business. Prior to 2007, if your taxable sales were $500,000 or less, Canada Revenue Agency would have assigned an annual reporting period for your business. For fiscal years starting after 2007, you will be able to file an annual GST return if the total amount of your taxable sales are $1,500,000 or less. It is important to note that if you currently file a quarterly return and your taxable sales are below the $1,500,000 threshold, you will continue filing a quarterly return unless you choose otherwise. Therefore, if you would like to reduce the number of times you have to file a GST return down to once a year, you will have to contact CRA and request that this change be made. One thing to keep in mind though is that even if your business is below the $1,500,000 taxable sales figure, you can still opt to file a quarterly or even monthly GST return. There are times when filing on a more frequent basis may be advantageous.

TAX BEATER

Speed up Input Tax Credit refunds by electing to file quarterly or monthly.

If you are in a business that is generating consistent GST refunds, you may want to consider electing to file your GST return on a quarterly or monthly basis. For example, if the majority of your sales are export sales or you are a farmer or fisherman with zero-rated taxable sales, then it is likely you will be generating GST refunds on a regular basis. If you file annually, you will get that refund only at the end of the year. If you move to a quarterly or monthly filing system, you will speed up the GST refunds. This will help the cash flow in your business.

The trade off with speeding up the GST refunds is, of course, having to file the GST returns more often. Although the forms are not that difficult to complete, whether the extra hassle is worth getting your money earlier is a personal judgement call.

If, on the other hand, you always have to remit GST, then there is no real advantage to speeding up the process. Filing once a year will be the simplest approach and will provide the least administrative burden. If you normally have to pay GST, the government will usually request that you make four quarterly instalments to prepay the next year's GST liability. Therefore, annual filing only provides some administrative savings. Often from a cash flow point of view there is no savings, as you are required to remit GST instalments on a quarterly basis.

If your taxable sales for the year are greater than $1,500,000 but less than $6,000,000, you will be assigned a quarterly reporting period. When your sales are in this range, you will not have the option of filing annually. Your income is too great. On the other hand, you will have the option of filing monthly.

TAX BEATER
Reduce hassles and reporting costs by filing GST returns only as required.

Once again, moving up to a monthly reporting period can make a lot of sense if your business is generating significant GST refunds. If your business is primarily selling to foreign countries or you are selling some other zero-rated product or service, then speeding up the GST refunds makes good business sense.

When Are the GST Returns Due?

If you are filing your GST return on an annual basis (unless you qualify for the exception noted below), the return is due, along with any remittance required, three months after the year-end of your business. If, as an annual filer, you are required to make quarterly instalments, the instalment is due one month after the end of your business quarter.

For example, if your business has a January year-end, the annual GST return will be due by April 30 and your first instalment will be due by May 31. April 30 would be the first quarter for your business year; therefore, your first instalment would be due one month after your first quarter, or May 31.

If you are required, or elect, to file your GST returns on a quarterly basis, you will be required to file your GST return, along with any remittance, if applicable, within one month after that quarterly reporting period. For example, if your year-end is December, your first quarterly reporting period will be from January 1 to March 31, and the return for the reporting period, along with any payment required, will be due by April 30.

If you are required, or elect, to file your GST returns on a monthly basis, you will be required to file your GST return, along with any remittance, if applicable, within one month after that monthly reporting period. So in this case, you will need to file the GST return for the month of January by the end of February and February's by the end of March and so on.

There is an exception for some to file their GST returns later if you can meet all of the following conditions. If you operate your business as a sole proprietor or in a partnership, you qualify and have elected to file your return on an annual basis and the fiscal year end of your business is December 31, then your GST will be due for filing by June 15th, just like your personal tax return. However, just like your personal tax return, any tax liability is due April 30 and CRA will charge interest from May 1 on any taxes not paid.

What Happens If I'm Late in Filing My GST Return?

TAX BEATER

Remit your GST on time and reduce the amount you pay.

Prior to April 1, 2007, if you owed GST to the government and were late in remitting the GST, CRA would charge you a penalty of 6% per year on any GST not remitted on time plus interest. As of April 1, 2007, a "failure to file" penalty will apply to any return you file late, unless there is a no amount owing, or if you are expecting a refund. This penalty is equal to 1% of the amount owing, plus 0.25% of the amount owing multiplied by the number of months the return is overdue, to a maximum of 12 months. Both the penalty and the interest are compounded daily.

In recent years new legislation has been passed relating to the deductibility of interest charged under the GST/HST portions of the Excise Tax Act. The purpose of this new legislation is to harmonize the rules related to the deductibility of fines and penalties for GST with those related to the deductibility of fines and penalties imposed by law, and by any government or agency. As a result, for taxation years beginning on or after April 1, 2007, any interest and penalties charged for outstanding GST amounts will no longer be deductible for tax purposes. Although these are the rules in place for taxation years beginning on or after April 1, 2007, you should remember that prior to this, both interest and penalties charged on late-filed GST returns and payments were tax deductible. So if your taxation year started on say January 1, 2007, you would still be eligible to deduct any interest and penalties charged on late-filed GST returns and payments.

If you are owed a refund, no penalty or interest will accrue, since there is no liability. In fact, if Canada Revenue Agency is slow in processing your refund, they will pay you interest on the amount you are owed. Up until April 1, 2007, interest on a refund was calculated beginning on the day that was 21 days after you filed your GST return for the current period, and any outstanding prior periods. Under new legislation, interest on a refund for a reporting period that ends on or after April 1, 2007, will be calculated beginning on the day that is 30 days after the later of:

- The day that the return in which the refund is claimed is filed with the CRA, and
- The day following the last day of the reporting period.

In addition to the new legislation surrounding the calculation of refund interest, there are also new restrictions on the payment of GST refunds. As of April 1, 2007, a GST refund will not be paid until all returns (including income tax returns) a business is required to file, have been filed with CRA at that time. That being said, also as of April 1, 2007, any refund owing to a business will not be paid if the business has any amounts owing for GST or income tax. In such cases, the GST refund may be automatically offset against the GST or income taxes owing. Clearly, the importance of filing your GST return on time cannot be understated!

It is still important to file your GST return on time, even if there is no activity. Filing your GST return on time, even if it is a "nil return" with no transactions, will ensure that future refunds are processed quickly and it will stop Canada Revenue Agency from mailing out to you a request for a GST return.

What Happens If My Customer Doesn't Pay His Account?

When you make a sale and invoice your customer, you must remit the GST on the sale for that reporting period, regardless of when you collect the account. For example, assume that you have a December year-end and you are filing your GST returns on a quarterly basis. In September you made a sale to a customer for $1,000 and charged the customer $50 in GST. You delivered your product and the customer agreed to pay in 90 days.

Since you are filing your GST returns on a quarterly basis, you will have to remit the $50 of GST collected, net of any input tax credits, one month after the end of your third quarter, or by October 31. The $50 must be remitted, even though you haven't collected the money from your customer.

If your customer doesn't pay the account and you write the account off as a bad debt, make sure you remember to deduct the GST written off on the next GST return. To do this, deduct the amount of GST not collected on line 107 of

TAX BEATER

Make sure all of the returns your business is required to file have in fact been filed in order to have your refunds processed quickly.

TAX BEATER

Remember to request a refund of the GST and PST on accounts receivable that you have written off.

the GST tax return. You have up to four years from the time you wrote off the bad debt to claim the GST. So you may want to review the accounts that you have written off over the past four years to ensure you claimed a refund of the GST.

Many provincial sales tax systems work the same way, requiring you to remit the provincial sales tax at the time a sale is made, not when the money is collected. Therefore, if you charged provincial sales tax on the sale, remember to apply for the refund of this tax as well. The time frame for going back and claiming a refund on old written-off accounts will vary from province to province. If you are considering reviewing your old files to claim a refund on an old bad debt, you should call your regional sales tax office to clarify the period within which your province will accept a late adjustment.

What If I Offer My Customer a Discount for Early Payment or Charge Interest on Late Payments?

The rules associated with offering your customers a discount are very complex. If you offer discounts, then you may want to seek help from your tax coach to make sure that you are calculating the GST correctly. Even though this discount may be small, over time and over many transactions, even small percentages can add up. Having said this, let's look at the general rules.

If you offer your customer a discount for making his or her payment early, you are required to charge GST on the full amount of the sale, even if your customer takes advantage of the discount. For example, if you invoice a customer $100 plus $5 GST with terms of a 2% discount if paid in 20 days, then, even though the customer may take the 2% discount, you must still remit the $5 of GST. At first look, this would appear unfair in that you collected less than the original invoice amount of $100 plus GST, yet you must remit based on the original invoice amount. However, this is how the legislation was enacted and this is what is required. The offset, however, is that you should be entitled to a GST input tax credit of 5/105 of the cash discount. This was supported recently in the Tax Court of Canada case, William E. Coutts Company Ltd. v. The Queen. So if you are offering customers discounts for early payments, make sure that you are remitting the correct amount of GST and obtaining all of the relief in the form of input tax credits that you are entitled.

With respect to charging interest on late payments, the rules are a lot easier to work with. If you charge your customers interest on late payments then you do not have to add GST on the interest charged. You would just charge interest based on the original invoice amount.

Do I Charge GST on the Sale of Used Capital Assets?

For whatever reason, selling used capital assets seems to cause more GST problems then any other area. It's likely because, with most businesses, a system is in place to capture the GST for all of the regular sales and purchases. But sales of old, used equipment don't happen every day. Thus, the GST is often forgotten.

TAX BEATER

Remember to charge GST on the sale of used capital assets.

As a GST registrant, you are required to charge GST on all sales in your business, which includes sales of used capital assets. Even though these sales are not typical for your business, you are still required to charge GST and remit the tax. So when you sell that old computer to your neighbour's child for $200, you have to charge $10 GST on the sale.

What Happens If I Give a Customer a Gift or a Free Product or Service?

TAX BEATER

Remember to claim ITCs on gifts or free samples you provide to your customers

If as a sign of appreciation, you provide a customer with a gift or a free product or service, you do not charge GST or HST on such items. You can however claim an input tax credit for the GST/HST you pay or owe on your purchases to provide these items so long as they relate to you commercial activities. For example, if you operate a hair salon and you wish to thank one of your customers for their loyalty over the years by giving them a complimentary bottle of shampoo, you would not collect GST or HST on this item. You would however claim an input tax credit for the shampoo that you purchased.

What Happens If a Customer Provides You With a Deposit?

If a customer provides you with a deposit for a good or service to be provided in the future, you do not collect GST/HST. GST/HST would be collected on the deposit when it is applied to the actual purchase price. However, if the customer does not make the purchase and loses the deposit, GST/HST must be calculated and remitted on the forfeited deposit. If the customer is registered for GST/HST they may be entitled to claim an input tax credit for the GST/HST paid on the forfeited deposit.

What Is the HST?

Effective April 1, 1997, the provinces of Nova Scotia, New Brunswick, and Newfoundland and Labrador (referred to as the "participating provinces") agreed to harmonize their provincial sales tax systems with the federal GST system. This single sales tax system is called the Harmonized Sales Tax or the HST.

TAX BEATER

Be careful to charge the HST on sales to participating pro-vinces or else you may be paying the tax.

The HST is essentially the same as the GST, with mainly the same rules applying to the same base of goods and services. Most of the complexities with the HST revolve around the fact that there are only three provinces participating in the HST and therefore rules have to be put into place for transactions occurring between provinces.

The HST tax rate is 13%, 5% going to the federal government and 8% going to the provinces. The federal government administers the HST providing some administrative relief to businesses as they only have to deal with one level of government and one system. The collection and input tax credit system is the same under the HST as the GST system with some minor exceptions in cross-provincial transactions and in the area of the simplified accounting methods. Overall, the HST is the same as the GST, only with a new name and a new rate.

Do I Have to Register for the HST?

No. If you were registered for the GST then you will automatically be registered for the HST. This is the case even if you reside in a non-participating province. All registered businesses across Canada were automatically registered for the HST effective April 1, 1997.

I Reside in a Participating Province. How Will the HST Affect My Business?

If you reside in a participating province and you are registered for the HST, you will be required to charge 13% on all taxable sales made to customers or all services provided to customers in your province or another participating province. If you make a sale to a customer in a non-participating province, then you would only charge 5% GST on that sale and the shipping costs associated with that sale. If your customer was picking up their purchase at your premises and shipping it themselves, then you would charge 13% HST on the sale since the ownership of the goods changed hands at your premises, which is in a participating province.

Similar to the GST system, as a registrant, you would be eligible to claim input tax credits on the HST that your business paid. As a result, for most businesses, the HST is tax neutral. When reporting the HST, you will generally not be required to identify the federal and provincial components of the HST separately. You will also be able to use the same GST forms under the HST system as under the old system.

I Reside in a Non-Participating Province. How Will the HST Affect My Business?

Even though you may not be a resident in one of the participating provinces, you may still be affected by the HST. If you sell taxable goods to a customer resident in a participating province and you are considered to own the goods until they reach your customer, then you will have to charge and collect the 13% HST on the sale of the goods and the shipping costs. On the other hand, if you sell goods to that customer in the participating province and they pick up the goods at your premises, then you will only have to charge 5% GST and any provincial tax as appropriate.

If you purchase goods from a participating province for use in a non-participating province, you should not be charged the 13% HST. If you are charged the 13% HST either by mistake or because the goods were used in the participating province, then you are eligible for an input tax credit of the 13% subject of course to the normal eligibility requirements for input tax credits.

As can be seen, even though you may be a resident of British Columbia, Ontario, or any other non-participating province, the HST can still affect you. If you do not charge HST on sales to participating provinces, you may be liable for the unremitted HST. So be careful when making sales to the east coast and remember to charge the proper amount of tax or else the taxman may win this round.

365 Days to Save

Many times a client will come into my office to discuss how to save taxes. The client will want to talk about complex corporate reorganizations or fancy uses of trusts. Once I sit down with them and discuss what's involved and the costs of these plans, they often lose interest.

Then I ask if they paid their taxes on time last year, as I advised. I ask how they purchased that new car. And the answers I get make me shake my head. Many people are looking for the knockout punch, that one great plan that will shelter all their money from tax. Yet they forget that saving tax dollars occurs throughout the year by doing a lot of little things correctly, little things like filing their tax returns on time or making tax instalments.

When Is My Tax Return Due?

This should be one of the simplest questions going. *Everyone* knows that your tax return is due April 30 each year, unless the government gives us an extension due to April 30 falling on a weekend. How-ever, for self-employed individuals and their spouses, the tax return filing date became somewhat more complicated in 1995.

Starting in 1995, if you reported self-employment income on your tax return, you, and in most cases your spouse, could delay filing your tax returns until June 15. However, if any income taxes are owing on these returns, these taxes are due on April 30.

What this means is, unless you are really confident that you don't have a tax liability, you will have to complete your tax return by April 30 in order to calculate how much you owe to the government. And if you're going to complete your tax return to estimate your tax liability and pay your taxes by April 30, you might just as well file your return by April 30, too.

So it is not much of a filing extension. Since interest will be charged on any insufficient payment, as a general rule, I do not recommend making use of the filing deadline extension and instead recommend that you keep filing your tax return by April 30.

> **TAX BEATER**
>
> File your tax return and pay any balance owing by April 30 to avoid being charged interest.

Why Should I File My Tax Return on Time?

So few people realize that performing simple things like filing their tax returns when due can, over time, significantly increase a person's wealth. Consider two individuals, who both, every year, have to pay $6,000 when they file their tax returns in April. Taxpayer A files her tax return on time. Taxpayer B always procrastinates and doesn't get around to filing his tax return until September each year, after a nice relaxing summer. Say this goes on for 15 years, and over that 15-year period the average return on invested income is 8%. Taxpayer A will find herself in a much better position, in fact having as much as $38,000 more wealth, just by doing such a simple thing as filing her tax return on time. Why? Let me explain.

The government tries to discourage taxpayers from filing their tax returns late by charging interest and penalties. From the date your tax payment is late to the date it is paid, you are charged interest, compounded daily, at a rate set by the government. This interest rate is known as the prescribed interest rate. The rate is set quarterly and is based on the 90-day T-bill rate. For the calculation of the interest charged on late tax payments, the government adds an additional 4% to the base prescribed rate. For our example, we'll assume that the average interest rate to be charged over the 15 years will be 10%.

Since Taxpayer B doesn't file his tax return until September, he will be charged a penalty for late filing of 5% on the balance owing on the tax return, plus 1% for every complete month that the tax return is late, to a maximum of 17%. For repeat offenders, the penalty is double, 10% plus 2% for each complete month to a maximum of 20 months. The repeat offender penalty only kicks in if the taxpayer has been notified in writing to file a tax return.

In our example, this will mean that Taxpayer B will incur a penalty in the first year of 10% of the taxes outstanding, plus interest. In the second and subsequent years, the penalty will be 20%. Over the course of 15 years, Taxpayer B will pay approximately $21,500 in penalties and interest. If this money had been invested, instead of being paid to the government, it could have accumulated to $38,000 before taxes. This example has been exaggerated to prove a point. Remember, you can "Beat the Taxman" in many ways, but often the most effective ways are the easiest.

> **TAX BEATER**
> Reduce the money you pay the government by paying and filing your tax return on time.

What Are Tax Instalments?

As a self-employed entrepreneur, you may be required to make income tax instalment payments. As your business becomes profitable, you will owe more tax. The government doesn't want to wait until the end of the year for you to pay that tax. So instead, they request that you make instalments periodically throughout the year. Essentially, they are asking you to prepay your tax for the current year.

This is not uncommon. Employees do the same thing, only it is less painful. Their employer withholds a portion of their pay and remits it on their behalf to the government. The employee is effectively making tax instalments every time he or she gets paid. But they don't see the money, and since they don't have it to spend, making the instalment is not as difficult. They may not like it, but it is not as painful.

As a self-employed entrepreneur, making this tax instalment can be annoying. However, as you will see, the alternative is worse.

Do I Have to Make a Tax Instalment?

Whether or not you have to make tax instalments for the upcoming taxation year depends on your tax liability that you are anticipating for the upcoming year and what has happened over the previous two years. If your net tax owing, not including instalments, for the upcoming year and either of the previous two years is greater than $3,000 (greater than $1,800 in Quebec), then you will be required to make instalments in the next year.

For example, if in 2007 your net tax owing was say $4,000 and you anticipate that in 2008 your net tax owing will be greater than $3,000, then you will be required to make instalments for 2008.

If you are a resident of Quebec, your net tax owing is defined as your federal tax payable minus your federal tax deducted at source, your refundable Quebec abatement and your refundable credits.

If you are a resident anywhere else in Canada, your net tax owing is defined as your federal and provincial taxes payable minus your tax deducted at source and your refundable tax credits.

The net tax owing also includes any liability for the Canada Pension Plan (except Quebec residents).

When Are the Tax Instalments Due?

Tax instalments are due every March 15, June 15, September 15, and December 15 of the year. Farmers and fishermen have until December 31 to make their instalment.

If you are required to make instalments, Canada Revenue Agency will mail you a reminder around February and August of each year.

Why Should I Make Tax Instalments?

Tax instalments appear to be a considerable hassle. So why should you make the instalments? Well, consider this. If you do not make your instalments on time or you do not remit sufficient instalments, Canada Revenue Agency will assess you interest on the insufficient payment. This means that you will be borrowing from the government. And their interest rate is normally higher than what the bank would charge.

Not only is the interest rate charged by the government higher than the bank rate, it is also not tax deductible. Had you borrowed from the bank to finance your business operations and thereby paid your tax instalments on time, you would have been eligible to deduct the interest expense and you would have saved tax dollars. However, interest paid to the government is not tax deductible. Using the government as a "bank" results in a significantly higher cost of borrowing!

AN EXAMPLE OF THE HIGH COST OF BORROWING FROM THE GOVERNMENT

Assumptions:

- Tax Liability of $15,000 outstanding for one year
- Average interest rate charged by the government, say 7%
- Average interest rate charged by the bank, say 4%
- For the purposes of this example, interest is calculated on a simple interest basis

Alternative 1—Borrow from Government	$
Taxes outstanding for one year	15,000
Interest rate charged	7%
Interest paid and cost to the business	1,050

Alternative 2—Borrow from Bank

Bank loan outstanding for one year	15,000
Interest rate charged	4%
Interest paid	600
Tax deduction at 46% rate	(276)
Cost to the business	324
Savings from Borrowing from the Bank	**726**

TAX BEATER

Pay your tax instalments as required to reduce your overall costs and increase profits.

And if this wasn't bad enough, Canada Revenue Agency will assess a penalty if the instalment interest charges exceed $1,000 in a year. And of course, this penalty is not tax deductible either. When these interest charges and penalties are added together, not making instalments can be a very costly way to finance your business.

AN EXAMPLE OF HOW THE INSTALMENT PENALTY WORKS

Assumptions:

- Instalment interest charged $3,000
- No instalments paid during the year

	$
Penalty equals 50% of	
a) Instalment interest charged	3,000
Minus the greater of:	
b) $1,000 and	(1,000)
c) 25% of the instalment interest you would have paid if you had made no instalments during the year (25% of $3,000 or $750)	
	2,000
	50%
Instalment Penalty	**1,000**

What Are My Instalment Options?

You have three options to choose from in any one year to calculate the amount of your instalments. In some years, this can be very important in minimizing the amount of money you pay to the government and maximizing your cash flow. Remember, effective tax planning includes deferring as long as possible the money you pay to the government. Making proper use of your instalment options is key to effective tax planning.

No-Calculation Option

Your first option, which is also the option that is automatically used by the government, is the "Second Preceding Year Option" or as Canada Revenue Agency calls it, the "No-Calculation Option." If you are required to make tax instalments, Canada Revenue Agency will notify you with reminder notices in February and August of each year. These reminder notices will indicate the amount of the tax instalment that you need to make to avoid any instalment interest charge. Canada Revenue Agency uses the no-calculation option to calculate the instalments required on these reminder notices. This method of calculating the instalments is as follows:

- The March 15 and June 15 instalment is based on your second preceding taxation year. For example, your March 15 and June 15, 2009, tax instalments will be based on one-quarter of your net tax owing and any Canada Pension Plan (CPP) or Quebec Pension Plan (QPP) for the *second preceding tax year*, or in this case 2007.

- The September 15 and December 15 instalment is meant to be a catch-up payment. The idea is that by December 15 you will have paid to the government in instalments the amount of your net tax liability *of the previous year*. With that in mind, the government calculates your remaining two instalments by first deducting your March 15 and June 15 instalments from *your prior year's net tax liability*. This balance is then divided by two to arrive at your last two instalment payments.

AN EXAMPLE OF HOW THE "SECOND PRECEDING YEAR INSTALMENT OPTION" WORKS

Assumptions:

- Net tax owing for 2007 was $3,000
- Net tax owing for 2008 was $5,000

Question:

What are my required tax instalments for 2009 under the "Second Preceding Year Option"?

Date of Instalment	Calculation of Instalment	$
March 15, 2009	$3,000 ÷ 4	750
June 15, 2009	$3,000 ÷ 4	750
September 15, 2009	$5,000 – $750 – $750	
	= $3,500 ÷ 2	1,750
December 15, 2009	$5,000 – $750 – $750	
	= $3,500 ÷ 2	1,750
Total Instalments Paid		**5,000**

TAX BEATER
Follow the "No-Calculation Option" when your income is stable or rising to minimize the amount of pre-paid tax.

Admittedly, this process is complicated, especially for something that should be as simple as making instalments. However, the system used prior to this one required you to make a March 15 instalment based on the net tax liability of the previous year which was due for filing on April 30—after the instalment was due. You were being asked to make an instalment before you were required to file your tax return which was used to calculate the instalment. And if you miscalculated the payment, you were charged interest!

The calculation of this instalment option is by far the most complicated. However, the nice thing is that you really don't need to understand how it is calculated. The more important thing to remember is this rule: If your income is stable or rising, you're better off using the "Second Preceding Year Option." Otherwise, consider one of the other two instalment options.

The other nice thing is that provided you pay the instalments on time as indicated on the instalment reminders sent by Canada Revenue Agency, you will not be charged instalment interest. This is the case even if Canada Revenue Agency has made an error in your favour when calculating the instalment amounts or have in error informed you that you do not need to make any instalments. By following this method, you should never have to worry about paying instalment interest.

Prior-Year Option

The second instalment option is often referred to as the "Prior-Year Option." With this option you make instalments based on one-quarter of your prior year net tax owing. For example, if you are calculating your 2009 instalment contributions, then you would take your 2008 net tax owing, including any CPP contributions payable, and divide this by four. This will provide you with four equal instalment payments for the year.

TAX BEATER
Increase cash flow by electing to use alternative instalment options.

This instalment option can be very useful in years where your income is decreasing. For example, assume that Jane had a net tax liability in 2007 of $20,000. It was an excellent year, in which she won several major contracts. However, in 2008 she didn't have such a great year, which resulted in a net tax liability of only $6,000.

In calculating her year 2009 instalments if she followed the second preceding year option as calculated by the government, she would make instalments of $5,000 on both March 15 and June 15 and then no instalments in September or December. Under the prior-year option, Jane could have made instalments of $1,500 on each of the four instalment dates, March 15, June 15, September 15, and December 15. By electing to use the prior-year option, Jane would have paid $4,000 less to the government and would have delayed paying the instalments longer.

Current-Year Option

The third and last instalment option is referred to as the "Current-Year Option." This option is similar to the prior-year method in that the instalments are equal throughout the year. However, instead of basing the instalments on the net tax liability of the prior year, the instalments are based on your estimate of your current year net tax liability.

This instalment option is extremely useful in years where you have a drop in income. For example, assume Jane had that really exceptional year in 2007 and had a net tax liability of $20,000. However, 2008 isn't shaping up to be a repeat year. Instead, she estimates that her net tax liability will be around $6,000.

If Jane used the prior-year instalment method, she would pay $5,000 on each of the four instalment dates. She would pay $20,000 over the course of the year, representing a significant cash drain on her business in a year that she is not doing as well.

Instead, if Jane estimates her next year properly and elects to use the current-year method, she could reduce her instalments from $20,000 for the year to $6,000 without being charged instalment interest. This is a significant improvement in cash flow, which, over time, will help to increase Jane's personal wealth.

A word of caution if you elect to use either the prior-year or current-year instalment options: If you incorrectly calculate your instalments or estimate your current year's tax liability incorrectly, and you do not remit enough in instalments during the year, Canada Revenue Agency will charge you late instalment interest and possibly penalties. To assist you in calculating your proper instalments, you should consider using Canada Revenue Agency's form T1033-WS, "Worksheet for Calculating YYYY Instalment Payments." It will greatly assist you in deciding which option is best for you.

What If I Miss a Tax Instalment?

Missing a tax instalment payment is just like borrowing money at a very high interest rate. This can be very costly to your business. So your objective should always be to make timely tax instalments. However, say, due to cash flow problems, procrastination, or simple forgetfulness, you missed one or two instalments. You can still reduce or eliminate any non-deductible interest charged by the government by prepaying your next instalment.

For example, say you miss your March 15th instalment. You can eliminate most or all of the instalment interest charge by paying to the government an amount equal to the total of the March 15th, June 15th, and September 15th instalments on June 15th. By prepaying your September 15th instalment, Canada Revenue Agency will offset the interest you earned on the prepayment against the interest you were charged on the late March 15th instalment.

Note, however, that prepaying your instalments will not earn you interest income. If you prepay your instalment, Canada Revenue Agency will not pay you interest income, they will only reduce any instalment interest they were going to charge you for the year. Therefore, in the above example, if the September 15 instalment is substantially greater than the March 15 instalment, it isn't worth it to prepay the entire September instalment. Instead, only prepay an amount equal to the March instalment you missed.

> **TAX BEATER**
>
> If you miss an instalment payment, catch up your instalments and prepay the next instalment to reduce or eliminate the non-deductible instalment interest charge.

What Is the Penalty for Forgetting to Remit Employee Deductions on Time?

If you have employees in your business or hire a family member to help you, remitting tax withholdings, CPP/QPP, and EI (Employment Insurance) payments on time is an integral part of reducing every day the money you pay to the government. By neglecting to remit these taxes on time, you increase the amount of money you pay to the government through increased interest and penalty payments.

Prior to July 2003, failure to withhold and remit tax, CPP/QPP, and EI for your employees resulted in a 10% penalty of the amount not remitted for each occurrence. For the second occurrence in the same year, the penalty could increase to 20% of the amount not remitted, if the failure to remit was made knowingly, intentionally, or due to gross negligence. And of course, these penalties will not be tax deductible.

Effective after June 2003 the government introduced a graduated system of assessing penalties for late remittance of employee deductions. The new rules are slightly more lenient for employers who are only late by a few days. With the new system, if you are late by three days or less, a penalty of 3% will apply. If you are four or five days late, the penalty will be 5%. Six or seven days late will result in a 7% penalty. Once you reach eight days late, then the 10% penalty will apply. If you fail to remit the employee deductions, then the 10% full penalty will also still apply. As well, if your failure was made knowingly or under circumstances amounting to gross negligence then the 20% penalty can still apply. While the new graduated system is certainly less punitive when honest mistakes occur, the bottom line is that remitting employee deductions on time is still the least costly method for your business.

When Are Employee Remittances Due for Filing?

If your average monthly payroll remittances for your second preceding calendar year were less than $15,000 per month, you must make your remittances by the 15th of the month following the month in which your payroll is paid. For example, if the current year is 2008, to determine your filing due date, you would look at what your average monthly payroll remittances were for the calendar year 2006. If the average monthly remittances were less than $15,000 per month, your due date for payroll remittances is the 15th of the month following the month your employees were paid.

As of January 1, 2008, if your average monthly withholdings were less than $3,000 for either the first or second preceding calendar year *and* you have a perfect compliance record for the preceding twelve months, then you would be eligible to remit on a quarterly basis. (Prior to 2008, you were

Average Monthly Remittance for Second Preceding Year	Frequency and Timing of Remittance
Less than $3,000/month and a perfect compliance record	15th of the month following the end of the quarter's of March, June, September, and December
Less than $15,000/month	15th day of the month following month in which payroll paid
Greater than $15,000/month and less than $50,000/month	1. Payroll paid before 16th day of the month, remittance due on or before 25th day of the month. 2. Payroll paid after 15th day of the month, remittance due on or before the 10th day of the following month.
Equal to or greater than $50,000/month	Remittance due by third day (not including Saturday, Sunday or holiday) after the end of the following periods in which the payments were made: 1. Period beginning on the 1st day and ending on the 7th day of the month. 2. Period beginning on the 8th day and ending on the 14th day of the month. 3. Period beginning on the 15th day ending on the 21st day of the month; and 4. Period beginning on the 22nd day and ending on the last day of the month.

TAX BEATER

Properly withhold and remit payroll taxes on time.

eligible to remit on a quarterly basis if your average monthly withholdings were less than $1,000.) CRA considers employers to have a perfect compliance record when all deductions, withholdings, and remittances of income tax, GST/HST, CPP contributions, and EI premiums have been made on time and T4 information returns and GST/HST returns are also filed on time. Quarterly remittance periods would end on March 31, June 30, September 30, and December 31, and the remittances would be due by the 15th of the month following the end of the quarters.

If your average monthly payroll remittances for the second preceding calendar year were greater than $15,000 per month, the payroll remittances are more frequent. Most small business and home-based entrepreneurs are not likely to have this large a payroll. However, if you do fall into this category, see the table on the previous page for the frequency of the remittances.

TAX BEATER

Increase cash flow and save time by electing to reduce your payroll remittance frequency.

If your payroll has been dropping such that you have gone below the $15,000 per month threshold, you can elect to make remittances based on the level of average monthly payroll remittances of the prior year, instead of the second preceding year. For example, if in 2007 your average monthly payroll remittances were $16,000, and in 2008 your average payroll remittances were $13,000, normally you would still be required to make payroll remittances twice a month. Under normal circumstances you must look back to 2007 to determine your frequency of remittances for 2009.

However, you can elect to reduce your remittance frequency to once a month by advising Canada Revenue Agency that you are electing to base your 2009 remittances on your 2008 average monthly payroll remittances. This should provide greater cash flow and fewer administrative hassles.

TAX BEATER

File employee information returns by the end of February to avoid significant penalties.

When Are Employee Information Returns Due for Filing?

As an employer, you are responsible for filing employee information returns, such as T4 Short, T4, T4A, and T4F Supplementary and Summaries as appropriate. These forms are due for filing on or before the last day of February for the previous calendar year. If you delay in preparing these forms, the penalty can be quite steep. Canada Revenue Agency will charge you a penalty of $25 a day for each failure to file the above information returns, with a minimum penalty of $100 to a maximum penalty of $2,500. And, of course, these penalties are not tax deductible.

You are also responsible for making a reasonable attempt at obtaining the Social Insurance Number (or SIN) of your employees. Evidence of a reasonable attempt would generally include a copy of a letter to your employee asking for their SIN. If you do not make a reasonable effort to obtain SINs for your employees, Canada Revenue Agency may charge you $100 for each employee for whom you do not have a SIN.

> **TAX BEATER**
>
> Make a reasonable effort to obtain employee SINs or be charged a penalty.

What is the Contract Payment Reporting System?

In an effort to combat the underground economy, effective January 1, 1999 the government introduced the mandatory Contract Payment Reporting System. The main purpose of the system is to encourage members of the construction industry to report their income. The system encourages this by requiring construction businesses to record payments they make to subcontractors who provide construction services. The construction businesses then have to report these payments to CRA. The reporting system is for information purposes only, meaning that the subcontractors do not have to reconcile the reporting information with the income they report on their tax returns. In fact, the construction business does not even have to inform the subcontractor of the details of the amounts being reported. The system is intended to provide CRA with information that they can use to ensure the subcontractors are filing their tax returns with reasonable amounts of income being reported.

The contract payment reporting system is applicable to individuals, partnerships and corporations whose primary business activity is construction and who make payments to subcontractors for services performed. The system is only focused on services, not goods that are sold. If there is a mixture of goods and services, then you only have to report if the service component is greater than $500. This means that if 50% or more of your business activity is in the area of excavation, erection, installation, alteration, modification, repair, improvement, demolition, destruction, dismantling, or removal of any structure or part, including but not limited to buildings, roads and bridges, then the reporting system will apply to you.

The information that needs to be reported includes the subcontractor's name, address, identification number (such as their GST number, CRA business number or social insurance number), the amount of the contract payments, and the reporting period to which the payments relate (either calendar year or your fiscal year). The information can be submitted using the T5018 Information Return package or by simply sending to CRA a tabular worksheet with the required information going across the page with one line for each subcontractor. The information must be submitted within six months of the end of your reporting period. The key is to ensure that if you are required to submit the information, that you do so. If construction businesses do not submit the required information, they can be assessed penalties.

TAX BEATER

If required, submit contract payment information to CRA to avoid being assessed penalties.

What Fines and Penalties Are Tax Deductible?

The rules relating to the deductibility of fines and penalties changed in late 1999 due to an egg producer in British Columbia. 65302 British Columbia Limited was charged an over-quota levy from the B.C. Egg Marketing Board and attempted to deduct this levy on their tax return. Canada Revenue Agency decided that the penalty should not be tax deductible in accordance with the interpretations they had developed over time and disallowed the deduction. The taxpayer took CRA to court and the case went all the way to the Supreme Court of Canada.

The majority ruling of the Supreme Court of Canada decided in favour of the taxpayer; the penalty should be tax deductible. The court went on to say that all fines and penalties, except those specifically denied by the *Income Tax Act*, are tax deductible if they were incurred to earn income.

This is a significant departure from how the courts and CRA have been treating fines and penalties in the past. Previously, CRA would look at whether or not the fine or penalty was levied because the infraction was contrary to public policy. This meant that CRA would be making value judgements on what is contrary to public policy and what is not. This has over the years generated many court cases as not everyone has the same opinion regarding public policy. The Supreme Court felt this was inappropriate and that CRA should not be making public policy decisions. This should be left to parliament. So it falls to the Income Tax Act. If the fine or penalty is not specifically dealt with in the Income Tax Act and was incurred to earn income, the fine or penalty would be tax deductible.

The court did however state that there could be some extreme circumstances where a fine or penalty imposed could not be considered incurred for the purpose of producing income. In this case, even though an argument could be made the fine or penalty was for the purpose of producing income, the crime or infraction would be so repulsive it would be deemed not for the purpose of producing income and therefore not tax deductible.

As mentioned above, the Supreme Court of Canada felt it was inappropriate for CRA to be making policy decisions and that this should be left to the government in the form of legislation. The government listened to these comments and in 2004 made changes to the legislation, such that fines and penalties will no longer be tax deductible. Specifically any penalties incurred after March 22, 2004 that were imposed by law, by any government or agency, would no longer be tax deductible. In addition to this, for taxation years beginning on or after April 1, 2007, similar rules regarding the deductibility of fines and penalties imposed by law and by any government or agency apply to fines and penalties imposed under the Excise Act, the Air Travellers Security Charge Act, and the GST/HST portions of the Excise Tax Act.

So, what does this mean? It means that penalties imposed before March 22, 2004 that were incurred to earn income will be tax deductible, unless specifically denied by the Income Tax Act. For the most part this will only deny penalties imposed under the Income Tax Act, any of the Provincial Income Tax Acts and the GST/HST portions of the Excise Tax Act. All other penalties that were imposed in the process of earning income would be for the most part deductible, unless the infraction was so egregious or repulsive that the fine or penalty could not have been considered incurred in the process of earning income. For penalties imposed after March 22, 2004, the deductibility has become much more restrictive. Essentially, other than the exceptions noted above, no penalty will be tax deductible in your business.

> **TAX BEATER**
>
> Reduce the sting of infractions by knowing which fines and penalties are tax deductible.

How Can I Maximize My Deductible Interest?

For interest paid on borrowed money to be tax deductible, the loan must be for business reasons. It is not sufficient to say that 100% of your mortgage interest is tax deductible because you had enough savings to pay off the mortgage and then borrowed for your business. In order to make that interest tax deductible, you need to actually pay off your mortgage and then borrow for your business.

This is an area that Canada Revenue Agency does watch quite closely. Many court cases have dealt with the issue of interest deductibility. And it is very clear that for a loan to be deductible, the loan *must* have been taken out for business purposes.

> **TAX BEATER**
>
> Turn personal loans into business loans and deduct the interest for tax purposes.

So, how can you maximize your deductible interest? Well, one way is exactly how I described above. If you have savings that you were going to use in your business and you have a mortgage or a personal car loan still outstanding, consider using your savings to pay off those loans. Then borrow what you need for the business, and use the house or car as security to obtain a lower interest rate. You will be in the same position as before, except now the interest will be tax deductible.

> **TAX BEATER**
>
> Pay down personal loans before business loans to maximize your tax-deductible interest expense.

Consider also the situation where you have two loans. One is a business loan, where the interest is tax deductible. The other is a personal loan where the interest is not tax deductible. In most cases it will make more sense to pay off the personal loan first, before reducing the business loan. This will allow you to maximize your tax deductible interest expense.

Can I Deduct the Cost of Life Insurance?

Generally speaking, as a small-business entrepreneur, you cannot deduct the cost of life insurance. However, you may be able to arrange your affairs in such a way to make your life insurance premiums deductible.

> **TAX BEATER**
> Structure business loans to turn non-deductible insurance premiums into tax-deductible expenditures.

In order for life insurance premiums to be tax deductible, the life insurance policy must be used as security for a business loan. In addition, the lender must require that the policy be used as security, the lending institution must be a Canadian bank, trust company, credit union, insurance company, or corporation whose principal business is lending money to strangers, *and* the interest on the loan must be normally tax deductible.

By structuring your bank borrowings to take advantage of these restrictions, it may be possible to turn a non-deductible expense into a tax deductible expenditure.

As a Self-Employed Entrepreneur Can I Deduct Health and Dental Premiums?

Until recently, as a self-employed entrepreneur, you were not eligible to deduct health and dental premiums. Then in the February 1998 budget the government announced that for 1998 and future taxation years, health and dental premiums will be deductible by the self-employed. The government will also now allow the deduction of health and dental premiums to corporations for the payments made on behalf of the owners of the company.

If you're thinking that this sounds too simple, then congratulations, you're right. There are a number of restrictions

TAX BEATER

Deduct your health and dental premiums in your business and save.

which may prevent your deduction of the health and dental premiums. For most, these restrictions will not be a concern. However, some might find them to be a problem.

The first restriction is that you can only deduct health and dental premiums in your unincorporated business provided that you are actively involved in the business and either the business is your primary source of income in the current year or your income from other sources does not exceed $10,000. For the business to represent your primary source of income, generally that means that more than 50% of your income is derived from your business.

Another restriction is that in order to deduct the health and dental premiums, you must offer equivalent coverage to all permanent full-time arm's-length employees. (Arm's-length employees are employees that are not related to you by blood, marriage, or adoption.) You will also be restricted to deducting a maximum of $1,500 for each, yourself and your spouse, and $750 per child. This limit does not apply where the number of arm's-length employees receiving coverage represents at least one-half of the total number of employees in the business. You can also only deduct premiums that are purchased from a third party normally in the business of selling insurance, or the health and dental plan is operated by a trustee that is in the business of operating such plans. And lastly, where you deduct the costs of your health and dental plan in your business, you will not be eligible to claim a medical expense tax credit for the payments.

Although the rules are complicated, the benefits can be significant. The tax savings from deducting your health and dental premiums in your business could amount to half the cost of your premiums, making this a clear win for the taxpayer.

As a Self-Employed Entrepreneur Can I Deduct CPP/QPP Contributions?

There are a number of small inequities that have existed in the tax laws in relation to the deduction of certain expenses for a self-employed entrepreneur in comparison to the same expenses for his or her employees. The deduction of health and dental premiums is one such example that was corrected in 1998. Starting in 2001, for businesses that had a taxation year ending after 2000, the deduction of Canada Pension Plan or Quebec Pension Plan contributions also became more comparable with regular employees. Self-employed entrepreneurs are now permitted to deduct one-half of Canada Pension Plan or Quebec Pension Plan contributions paid for their own coverage. The non-deductible half will continue to qualify for a tax credit.

This treatment closer approximates the tax treatment afforded to other employees of the business. With normal employees, the business deducts their portion of the CPP/QPP paid on behalf of the employee. The employee then claims a tax credit on their tax return for the amount that they pay. With the self-employed, under the old rules the employer and employee's portion of the CPP/QPP could only be claimed as a tax credit. Now one half will be deductible and one half will be treated as a tax credit.

> **TAX BEATER**
> Deduct one-half of CPP/QPP contributions and save.

The distinction is small but important. As a deduction from income, the expense can be claimed using the tax rate stairway (see Round 4). So if your business is profitable and you are in the highest tax level, then the CPP/QPP deduction will save approximately 46 cents on the dollar. As a tax credit, the maximum tax savings is only about 25 cents on the dollar. Being able to deduct CPP/QPP contributions provides a much greater chance to save tax dollars.

How Much Can I Deduct for Meals, Beverages, and Entertainment Expenses?

In order for meals, beverages, and entertainment expenses to be tax deductible they must have been incurred to earn business income. And then, only 50% of the meals, beverages, and entertainment expenses can be deducted on your tax return. Taking your spouse out for dinner to make up for some late business meetings would not qualify as a business expense. It might be a nice thing to do, but would not normally be tax deductible. On the other hand, taking a business client out for dinner in the hopes to land that contract would normally meet the business test and 50% of the meal would be tax deductible.

An exception to this rule would be any meal, beverage, or entertainment expenses that are available to all employees, where you have employees. For example, if you have a Christmas party, the cost of the party would be fully deductible since all of the employees would be eligible to attend. Even if all of the employees did not attend, as long as they were all invited, 100% of the cost of the Christmas party would be deductible. A change in the February 24, 1998 budget restricts the number of events that are fully deductible to six in any calendar year.

TAX BEATER

Deduct 100% of meal costs at Remote Work Sites.

Be aware, however, that you are not able to deduct any meal costs associated with you or an employee eating at a local restaurant within your metropolitan area, unless you're entertaining a client or there was some good business purpose. You are not able to deduct the cost of eating daily at the local diner or grabbing a sandwich at the deli. Again, there must be a business purpose to the expense.

A change in the rules in the February 24, 1998 budget made it easier for employers to deduct 100% of the meal costs provided at "remote" work sites. The new definition of remote work site is any location that is at least 30 kilometres from the nearest urban area of at least 40,000 people, where the employee is not expected to return daily to his or her principal residence. Previously, Canada Revenue Agency interpreted a remote work site as a location at least 80 kilometres from the nearest established community of more than 1,000 people. So if you are providing meals for your employees in an area that would meet the interpretation of remote work site, make sure you deduct 100% of the meal costs.

TAX BEATER

Maximize your meal expenses by keeping track of which meals are fully deductible.

You can also deduct 100% of the meal cost built into a rail, airplane, or bus ticket. However, if the ticket shows the cost of the meal separately, then you can only deduct 50% of the cost. As well, you can deduct the full cost of meals, beverages, and entertainment expenses if you pay and then subsequently bill your client. Your client would only be eligible to deduct 50%. You are expected however, to estimate the meal costs associated with conventions and deduct only 50%. Its hard to believe that going out for dinner could be so complicated.

Can I Deduct the Costs Associated with Entertaining Clients at a Club, Camp, Lodge, Yacht, or Golf Course?

Unfortunately, the government has taken a very strict view on entertaining clients, employees, suppliers, etc., at clubs, camps, lodges, golf courses, and on a yacht. Unless your business involves the ownership and renting of a club, camp, lodge, yacht, or golf course, as a general rule no deduction is permitted relating to the use of these facilities. Therefore, if you take your client out for a round of golf, you cannot deduct that round of golf in your business for tax purposes. Even though business may be discussed on the course and you may have even closed a deal, you cannot deduct the cost of the green fees or membership.

With the golf course green fees, the rules are very clear. Golf is considered a recreational activity and therefore the expenses related to that activity are not tax deductible. However, waters begin to get muddy when you look at what is a camp or a lodge. If you conduct a sales meeting for your employees, for example, at a downtown hotel which has very few recreational facilities but good meeting rooms for the meeting, then generally speaking the cost of the meeting would be tax deductible. On the other hand, if you conducted the same sales meeting at a fishing lodge, away from the hustle and bustle of the city, that had several recreational activities at the lodge, then the cost of the meeting generally would be denied. This obvious contradiction has been acknowledged and held up not only by Canada Revenue Agency but also by the courts.

To get the tax deduction for the sales meeting at the fishing lodge, you will need to prove to Canada Revenue Agency, should they ask, that there was a genuine business purpose for using the camp or lodge and prove that the purpose was not to entertain clients, suppliers, shareholders, or employees. How you might prove this will depend on the circumstances. Some suggestions would be to keep a detailed agenda of the meeting(s) including times, attendance, and material covered. Also request detailed bills that will indicate what services were used by your guests. If you're at a lodge where certain recreational facilities are provided free of charge, you won't be able to prevent you're guests from using these facilities. However, if you can prove that the majority of the time spent at the lodge was to deal with business issues, you should be successful in deducting its cost.

If you own a camp, lodge, cottage, or yacht and you occasionally entertain clients, suppliers, shareholders, or employees at your facilities, you would not be eligible to deduct the maintenance cost of the facilities. Canada Revenue Agency will only allow the deduction of costs associated with these facilities if there is a genuine business purpose. The entertainment of clients is not consider a genuine business purpose.

Can I Deduct the Cost of a Meal Before or After a Round of Golf?

With the entertainment of key clients, suppliers, and employees becoming such an important aspect of doing business, there appears to have developed an informal war between taxpayers and the government on what is an acceptable deduction concerning entertainment expenses. The latest clash has involved the deductiblity of meals at a golf course.

A few years ago, Canada Revenue Agency was asked if the cost of business meals at a golf course were deductible, subject to the 50% limitation. The department's response was that any meals or entertainment of clients, employees, suppliers, etc. at a golf facility were not tax deductible, just like the cost of the green fees themselves are not deductible. This lead to the unusual result that should you have had dinner at the restaurant across the street, the meal would be deductible, but in the golf course dining room, no deduction. No doubt many golf course owners were concerned and upset with this interpretation.

Well, Canada Revenue Agency reconsidered this interpretation and agreed to allow business meals and entertainment expenses incurred at a golf course to be tax deductible, subject to the 50% limitation. (The green fees remain non-deductible.) This is good news for both owners of businesses and the golf courses. Be aware, however, to ensure you get to deduct the cost of entertaining your clients, make sure that the meal and beverage expenses are clearly noted on your bill or receipt. If your receipt is all inclusive without a breakout of the cost for meals and beverages, Canada Revenue Agency will disallow the entire expense and you will have lost this contest with the taxman.

TAX BEATER

Itemize cost of meals and beverages at golf courses to ensure deductibility.

Can I Give a Tax-Free Gift to My Employees?

If you had an employee that did a really good job and you wanted to reward that employee with a little extra pay of say $500, then that bonus would be taxable as income to your employee and tax deductible to your business. However, you want to give your employee a little something extra but you would like for it not to be taxable to your employee. Can you just give them a gift and have it be non-taxable? The answer is yes, but you have to follow the rules or your gift will be taxable to your employee.

TAX BEATER

Consider non-cash gifts and awards to save your employee's some tax.

Starting in 2001, it is now possible to give two non-cash gifts and two non-cash awards per year per employee on a tax-free basis. The two non-cash gifts must be for special occasions such as Christmas, Hanukkah, birthdays, marriages, etc. The total cost of the gifts to the employer, including taxes, must not exceed $500 per year. In addition, two non-cash awards per year can be awarded in recognition of achievements such as reaching a milestone in years of service, meeting or exceeding safety standards, or other such accomplishments. Once again the total cost of the awards to the employer, including taxes, cannot exceed $500 per year. With gifts and awards, it is possible to provide employees with up to $1,000 tax free in non-cash recognition with the employer still being able to deduct the cost.

The key here is that the gift and/or award must be non-cash. If a cash or near-cash gift or award is given, then it will be considered a taxable benefit to the employee. Examples of near-cash gifts would include gift certificates, gold nuggets, or any items that can be easily converted into cash. In addition, if the cost of the gift(s) or award(s) exceeds $500, then the full fair market value of the gift or award will be included in the employee's income. And this $500 limit includes taxes. So be careful not to give cash or exceed the cost limit or else what you hoped would be a nice gesture on your part for your employee could become a very embarrassing and costly situation with the Taxman.

How Can I Maximize My Tax Savings on the Courses I Take?

It is surprising, but a simple thing like taking a course relating to your business can become very complex when you're determining how the course fees are treated for tax purposes. There are four alternative income tax treatments when it comes to course fees. Knowing these rules may assist you in deciding which course to take, if you have to choose among several.

The general rule relating to courses is that if the course is intended to maintain, update, or upgrade an existing skill that relates to your business, the costs associated with the course would be fully deductible. This means that if you are at the highest tax level, say at the 46% level, the course would be deductible at that rate.

If the course is taken to learn a new skill, the costs of the course are not fully deductible, but are instead treated as a capital expense. If the course relates to your business, you would be able to deduct over time a portion of the course as an eligible capital expenditure. (Eligible capital expenditure is discussed in more detail in Round 9.)

If the course did not relate to your business at all, the expenses would not be tax deductible, regardless of whether the course is developing a new skill or updating an existing skill.

The last possible tax treatment would be to claim the course as a tax credit on your personal tax return. If the course qualifies for a tuition tax credit, then Canada Revenue Agency takes the view that it must be claimed that way, despite the fact that the course may have been taken to upgrade an existing skill and be deductible as a business expense. By claiming the course as a tuition tax credit, you are eligible for tax savings of only approximately 25%. If the course was deductible in your business, then you could have received a tax savings of up to 46%.

In summary, if the course is eligible for the tuition tax credit, Canada Revenue Agency says you must claim it as a credit. If it is not eligible for the tuition tax credit and it relates to your business, then the costs can either be fully deducted as a business expense or deducted over time as an eligible capital expenditure, depending on whether the course is developing a new skill or not. If the course does not at all relate to your business and it is not eligible for the tuition tax credit, then it will not be tax deductible.

What Are the Tax Results If I Pay for an Employee's Training?

As an employer, if you pay for an employee's training, the training costs will normally be tax deductible. Additionally, in most cases, the training costs will not be taxable to the employee. Canada Revenue Agency has recently revised its guidelines on which type of employer-paid training would be subject to tax in the employees hands as a taxable benefit, and which would be added to the employee's T4. When an employer pays for training of personal interest or technical skills that are not related to the employer's business, then the costs for that training should be added to the employee's T4 as a taxable benefit.

TAX BEATER

Review your
employer-paid
training costs
to ensure your
staff are not
paying too much
tax.

On the other hand, courses that maintain or upgrade an employee's skills that relate to the employer's business would not be treated as a taxable benefit to the employee. As well, general employment-related and/or in-house training would also normally not result in a taxable benefit.

In summary, if you pay for an employee to finish a degree in a field related to the employee's current or future responsibilities in the employer's business, then the training costs would be tax deductible to the employer and not taxable to the employee. As well, other general business related courses like stress management, time management, first-aid, etc. would be deductible to the employer and not be taxable to the employee. However, that personal interest woodworking course paid by the employer may be deductible to the employer but would be taxable to the employee as a taxable benefit.

How Can I Maximize My Tax Savings on the Conventions I Attend?

Attending conventions is an excellent way to meet people with similar business interests, review the newest products, develop new customer contacts, and refresh your skills in your discipline. But if you're going to spend the money to attend a convention, you want to make sure that it will be tax deductible.

With tax savings in mind, there are a couple of things you should be aware of relating to conventions. First, you are allowed to deduct the costs of attending only *two* conventions a year. You should keep this in mind as you plan which conventions you want to attend.

Second, in order to deduct the costs of the convention, the convention must be for business purposes. This rules out your Star Trek convention, unless your business is selling Star Trek products!

Third, the convention must be held in an area that covers the geographical area of the organizer of the convention. This is meant to discourage a Canadian company from organizing a winter convention for Canadian business people in Florida.

However, it would be perfectly acceptable for you to attend a convention in Florida that was sponsored by a Florida company and related to your business interests in Canada.

You can save tax dollars by knowing which conventions will be allowed as a tax deduction before attending the convention. These decisions have to be made throughout the year, not in April when you're filing your tax return.

> **TAX BEATER**
>
> Know which conventions are tax deductible and attend accordingly.

Why Is Some of My Business Advertising Not Tax Deductible and How Can I Ensure 100% Will Be Deductible?

Despite the fact that you may advertise your product or service to a Canadian audience in a newspaper distributed in Canada, you may find that the advertising is not tax deductible. This can occur if one of the following (or other) restrictions apply: the newspaper you advertise in is not owned by Canadians; it is not edited by Canadian residents; it is not printed in Canada or the United States.

The idea here is that the government wants to encourage Canadians to buy Canadian. When we advertise to the Canadian public, the government wants us to use Canadian print media. They don't want us to use foreign newspapers to market primarily in Canada.

This relates also to television and radio advertising. Advertising expenses paid to U.S. radio and television stations that are primarily directed to the Canadian audience will not be deductible for tax purposes.

> **TAX BEATER**
>
> When advertising to the Canadian public, advertise with Canadian media to ensure your advertising dollars are tax deductible.

For magazines or periodicals, the rules are somewhat different. Effective for advertisements placed in periodicals after May 2000 you will be eligible for either 100% or 50% tax deduction depending on the original Canadian editorial content provided in the periodical. If the original Canadian editorial content is at least 80%, then you will be eligible for 100% tax deduction for your advertising dollars. If the original Canadian editorial content is less than 80% then you can deduct 50% of your advertising dollars even if the Canadian content is nil and the periodical is 100% foreign owned.

To ensure your advertising dollars are deductible, ask a few questions like: Who owns the paper? Where is the material printed? Where is the editing done? What is the original Canadian editorial content as a percentage of total content? If you're not getting satisfactory answers or you're still not sure, contact your local Canada Revenue Agency office. They should be able to tell you if your advertising dollars will be tax deductible.

What Are Some Year-End Tax-Saving Tips?

As I said at the beginning of the Round, saving tax dollars occurs 365 days a year. And one of those key days is the day you complete your tax return. The following are a couple of tax-saving tips to consider when you're filling out that T1 General form.

- **Value your inventory:** Consider writing off obsolete or damaged inventory, thereby reducing your taxes. If you sell products, and provided you are not using the cash method of accounting (see Round 2), then you must add up the value of your inventory at the year-end of your business. The value of your year-end inventory, or ending inventory, is not an expense to your business. It will become an expense when the product is sold.

  If you include in ending inventory obsolete and/or damaged goods, then you are deferring the tax deduction of those expenses. Instead, never include in ending inventory, obsolete, or damaged goods. This will maximize your tax savings.

- **Allow for your slow payers:** If you have clients who are slow in paying the money they owe you, allow for them. Provided you are not using the cash method of accounting, you will be required to include in your income the amounts your customers owe you, despite the fact that they have not paid you yet.

If you consider it doubtful that a particular customer will, in fact, pay you, why pay taxes on that revenue? Instead, allow for the receivable by not including it in your outstanding accounts receivable balance. This does not mean that you have given up collecting on the receivable. If the customer pays later, just include the amount paid in that year's income.

TAX BEATER

Provide for doubtful paying customers and defer tax dollars.

Home
Sweet Home

Operating your home-based business as a sole proprietor can provide many tax benefits. Deducting a portion of your home expenses is a goal for every home-based entrepreneur. In this Round we will look at the rules for deducting these home expenses.

Am I Eligible to Deduct Home Expenses?

The most publicized tax savings for home-based businesses is the deduction of home expenses. This is so attractive because it allows you to deduct costs that would normally not be tax deductible. In order to be eligible to deduct home expenses from your home-based business, you must meet one of the following criteria:

- your home must be your principal place of business; or

- you use a designated area in your home for the *sole* purpose of earning your business income, *and* you use this space on a regular and ongoing basis to meet clients.

For most home-based businesses, meeting these criteria is not a problem. However, for some businesses that have an office located outside the home, meeting these criteria may be more difficult. Where your home is not your principal place of business, ensure that you designate an area in your home to be used *solely* for your business. This means that the family room should not be used as your office, unless you're willing to kick everyone else out of that room. In addition, you must be prepared to meet clients in your office and be able to demonstrate to Canada Revenue Agency that you in fact do meet clients at home. By taking these extra steps, you can ensure that you can deduct home expenses in your business.

In most cases, however, the home-based entrepreneur's principal place of business will be the home. In this case, it is not necessary to conduct client meetings at home. However, in order to maximize the deduction of home expenses, you should still designate an area in your home to be used solely for business purposes. By doing so, you will maximize the deduction of home expenses. If you cannot designate an area to be used solely in your business, fear not, you can still deduct home expenses, just not as much.

How Do I Calculate the Home Expense Deductions?

If your principal place of business is at home, you can deduct a reasonable percentage of home expenses. How much you can deduct is usually determined by the following formula: divide the business area in your home by the overall square footage of your home, and multiply by the eligible expenses. For example, assume that you have converted the spare bedroom to be used solely in your business. If your spare bedroom has a floor space of 120 square feet and the total area of your home is 1,200 square feet, the amount of eligible home expenses that can be deducted is 120 divided by 1,200, or 10% of the eligible expenses.

If you cannot designate an area in your home for your business, you will have to pro-rate the approximate time the

TAX BEATER

If your home is not your principal place of business, designate an area in your home to be used solely for business purposes and conduct client meetings at home.

TAX BEATER

If your home is your principal place of business, maximize your tax deductions by designating an area in your home to be used exclusively for your business.

area is used for business purposes as compared to personal use. For example, assume you use the family room during the day while everyone else is either at work or school, and at night the room is once again used by the family. Say it works out that you use the room 60% of the time for business purposes. Assuming that the room represents 25% of the square footage of the house, you would be able to deduct 60% of 25%, or 15% of eligible home expenses.

You may be able to increase the business use of your home by including the hallway to your home office and front foyer. If you are meeting clients in your home, you will likely hang your clients coat up in the front foyer, your client will have to make use of the hallway to get to your office and to leave at the end of the meeting. In this case, more than just your office is being used for business purposes. Note that unless clients use a separate entrance to your home, you will have to estimate the amount of time the hallway and foyer are being used for business purposes in comparison to personal use. Remember, this proration of time that an area is being used for business use will only apply if your home is used as your principal place of business.

As can be seen from the way tax deductible home expenses are calculated, you can obtain tax savings by maximizing the area used in your business or reducing the area in your home. You can increase the area used in your business by making use of a larger room in your home for your business. A way to reduce the area of your home is to exclude, for example, your basement, if it is not usable living space.

> **TAX BEATER**
> Maximize the home area used in your business or minimize the area of your home.

What Kind of Home Expenses Can I Deduct?

Eligible home expenses include interest on your mortgage, house insurance, heat, electricity, water, maintenance and repairs to your home, property taxes, and any other general house expenses. A portion of any of these expenses can be deducted from your business income. In Quebec, these expenses are restricted by a further 50%.

Any expenses that relate directly to your business can be deducted 100% in your business. For example, if you have an increase in your insurance premium due to your business operations, you should deduct 100% of this increase.

Telephone and other consumable supplies are not considered home expenses and are therefore not subject to the area reduction. You can deduct a reasonable amount of these costs that relate to your business. For example, you can deduct a reasonable allocation of the line charge based on usage. Long distance charges that relate specifically to your business are tax deductible. If your business requires considerable use of the phone, you should consider having a separate telephone line for your business. This way, 100% of the phone costs will be tax deductible.

Are There Any Limitations on Deducting Home Expenses?

In the start-up years of many businesses, it is common not to make a profit. It often takes some time to establish your client base, to perfect your offering and generate sufficient sales to cover your costs. The low overhead you achieve by working at home helps, but is not always enough. It is important to realize that in deducting home expenses, you cannot create a loss or increase a loss through the deduction of home expenses.

For example, assume that after recording your direct business income and expenses (excluding home expenses) you have a net profit of $100. If the business portion of home expenses is $150, you would only be able to deduct $100 in the current year, bringing your net income to $0. The balance of $50 can be carried forward for as long as you are in business.

If your direct business income and expenses resulted in a net loss of $100 before deducting home expenses, you would not be able to deduct any home expenses, because you cannot increase the loss of $100 by deducting home expenses. However, these home expenses can be carried forward to be deducted in a future year where your business is profitable.

These rules provide some very important tax-saving ideas. First of all, even if your business is losing money and you cannot deduct the home expenses in the current year, you must keep track of those home expenses so that they can be deducted in a future year. Canada Revenue Agency is not going to deduct these expenses for you. It is up to you to record the information and deduct these expenses in a profitable year.

Another very important tax-saving technique that arises from these restrictions is to properly classify home expenses. With many expenses the distinction is clear. For example, property taxes relate to your home overall; therefore, the business portion is subject to the above restrictions. However, with other expenses the distinction may not be so clear-cut. For example, if you purchase a separate insurance rider for your business, you can deduct this cost, regardless of the above restriction, because it is a business expense. Or, if you increase your mortgage to help finance the start-up of your business, that portion of the mortgage interest that relates to the business is a business expense which you can deduct regardless of whether or not your business is profitable.

This distinction between expenses that are subject to the profitability test and those that are not is important, especially where you have other sources of income. If you are receiving a pension or have other sources of income, the maximizing of your business loss will significantly reduce the amount of tax you pay.

Can I Claim Moving Expenses?

Moving expenses normally consist of those expenses incurred when you leave your job in one city to start a new job in a new city. However, what if you are operating a business out of your home and you move the business and your home to a new city or at least 40 kilometres away from your previous residence? Can you claim moving expenses? The answer is possibly. The door has been opened a bit in this area thanks to the determination and patience of Mr. Charles Templeton who won his case to deduct moving expenses when he moved

TAX BEATER

Keep track of the business portion of home expenses so each year you can deduct them either in the current year or in a profitable year.

TAX BEATER

Maximize your tax savings by properly classifying the business portion of home expenses from business expenses.

his home-based business from Penetanguishene, Ontario, to Toronto.

Previous to this 1997 court decision, Canada Revenue Agency, and the tax courts for that matter, considered it necessary for an individual to move closer to their work location by at least 40 kilometres as determined by the shortest practical route. Therefore, if your workplace was in your home, you would not qualify for moving expenses since you did not move 40 kilometres closer. In fact, you would not have moved any closer at all. Your residence may have moved more than 40 kilometres, but you did not move 40 kilometres closer to your place of business.

In the Templeton case, the judge decided that it is appropriate for a taxpayer to claim moving expenses if he or she moves their home-based business and their home more than 40 kilometres from their previous location. Therefore, if you move your home-based business more than 40 kilometres in Canada, you may be eligible to claim moving expenses. The key however is that the move must be for business reasons with no significant personal element involved. CRA will be very skeptical that in fact the move is really only for personal reasons. So, in order to be able to deduct moving expenses you will need to clearly demonstrate that the move was primarily for business reasons.

TAX BEATER

If you have moved your home and your home-based business, consider claiming moving expenses and save.

What Moving Expenses Can I Deduct?

You can claim most reasonable expenses paid to move you and your family from your old residence to your new residence. These expenses can include:

- travelling costs, including meals and lodging for you and your family;

- transportation and storage costs for your household effects;

- temporary board and lodging for up to 15 days;

- costs associated with cancelling an unexpired lease at your former residence;

- costs associated with selling your former residence including advertising, notarial or legal fees, real estate commissions, and a mortgage penalty incurred because the mortgage was paid off before maturity;

- costs associated with purchasing a new home where you have sold or are selling an old home including taxes on transfer or registration of title and legal fees associated with the purchase of the new home.

You are not eligible to claim losses incurred as a result of the move or expenses incurred to make your previous home more saleable. In addition, you cannot claim moving expenses to the extent that you receive a reimbursement from any source.

Do I Need to Keep Receipts?

You must be able to support, if asked, all moving expenses with a receipt. And the tax department tends to keep a close eye on moving expenses and will often ask to see the receipts. There is an exception however, for meals and travel costs. Canada Revenue Agency now allows for an option of choosing either a detailed or simplified method to calculate the meal and travel costs for moving.

With the detailed method, you will need to keep all of your receipts to substantiate the claim. For meals this would mean keeping all of your restaurant receipts. For vehicle expenses it would mean keeping track of all vehicle costs for the year including fuel, oil, tires, license fees, insurance, maintenance and repairs, interest, and depreciation. You would also have to keep track of the number of kilometres you travelled for the move and the number of kilometres you travelled in the year. By dividing the number of kilometres you travelled for the move by the number of kilometres travelled in the year, you obtain a percentage you can use for all the vehicle expenses incurred in the year.

As you can see, the detailed method is very cumbersome when it comes to calculating travel expenses. The option provided by the government is to provide you with a flat expense for meals and travel. For 2006 and later years, the flat meal expense is $17 per meal, to a maximum of $51 per day, per person. No receipts are required.

For travel expenses, all you need to do is multiply the number of kilometres travelled in the year that related to the move and multiply this by the rate provided by the government. The rates vary from province to province (see table), so if you are moving from one province to the next, then the rate you use is the rate from the originating province. For example, if you moved from Ottawa to Montreal, then you would be able to claim mileage expense of 200 kilometres multiplied by the rate of 47 cents for Ontario, for a total of $95.40.

In deciding which method is best for you, the factors to consider include the number of kilometres required for the move, how high your operating and finance expenses are for your vehicle and whether or not you wish to keep track of all of the detailed information. For short moves, the simplified method is the most advisable. For long moves, then it may be more advantageous to use the detailed method.

Travel Rates for Moving, Medical and Northern Residents Deduction

British Columbia	48 cents/km
Alberta	48 cents/km
Saskatchewan	46 cents/km
Manitoba	46.5 cents/km
Ontario	49.5 cents/km
Quebec	52.5 cents/km
New Brunswick	47 cents/km
Nova Scotia	48 cents/km
Prince Edward Island	47 cents/km
Newfoundland & Labrador	50.5 cents/km

Northwest Territories	56.5 cents/km
Nunavut	56.5 cents/km
Yukon	58 cents/km

Rates in effect for 2007. 2008 rates were not available at the time of writing.

Are There Any Restrictions to Claiming Moving Expenses?

Canada Revenue Agency requires you to deduct moving expenses in the year you move. You can only deduct moving expenses to the extent of income that you receive at the new location. Therefore, if your business only generated income of $5,000 and your moving expenses were $8,000, you would only be able to deduct in the current year $5,000 of moving expenses. The remaining $3,000 can be carried forward one year and deducted against your business income in that year, assuming your business income is greater than $3,000.

TAX BEATER
Elect not to claim permissible deductions to increase your income so that you won't lose the ability to deduct moving expenses.

If you find that you run the risk of not being able to use up the moving expenses in either of the two years because your income is not sufficient enough, review your expenses in your business for expenses that you don't have to deduct. For example, consider not claiming capital cost allowance for one year so that you can maximize your moving expenses. Or alternatively, don't claim the reserve for doubtful accounts on some of your questionable accounts receivable. By doing so, your income will increase, hopefully enough to allow you to claim your moving expenses and then the following year you can go back to claiming CCA and the allowance for doubtful accounts.

If you are claiming moving expenses, complete form T1-M and submit it with your tax return. This form will assist you in making the moving expense claim as it details out most of the allowable expenses. It will also assist the tax department in determining your eligibility for moving expenses and will speed up the process of accepting the claim.

Capital vs. Expense: A Wealth of Distinction

One of the most important distinctions in tax, one that can result in significant tax savings if you get it right, is the distinction between a capital item and an expense item. If you make a mistake in this area and treat something as a capital expenditure instead of as an expense, you may find it will take five, ten, twenty years to fully deduct the cost of that purchase. Alternatively, being too aggressive and deducting capital expenditures as an expense could open you up to scrutiny from Canada Revenue Agency and reassessment. Finding that balance between capital and expense can be difficult, but the rewards are that you win Round 9 and definitely "Beat the Taxman."

What Is a Capital Expenditure?

Determining if a purchase should be capitalized or expensed will depend on many factors. With some purchases, it is clearcut. There is very little room for maneuvering. For example, when you purchase a building or a car, these are obviously capital purchases. However, what about replacing the roof on the house or placing a new engine in the car? Are these capital or expense purchases? There is no definitive answer to this question. Each situation must be reviewed on a case-by-case basis. In order to assist you in making the capital/expense distinction, I have laid out some of the general rules Canada Revenue Agency uses and examples for you to follow.

The first rule is whether or not the expenditure provides a lasting benefit—that is, can this item reasonably be expected to last a few years or more. If so, the expenditure will normally be considered a capital purchase. For example, the purchase of a computer provides a benefit to the business over a number of years and therefore should be a capital expenditure. The legal fees paid to incorporate a company will benefit the company for many years and, therefore, are considered a capital expenditure. Course fees paid to learn a new skill will benefit you for many years as you practise that skill, so they too are considered a capital expenditure.

The second rule is whether the expenditure is considered maintenance or an improvement. If the expenditure is merely restoring the property to its original condition, it would be considered an expense. For example, replacing a roof to bring the building back to its original condition is an expense. Replacing an old roof with a new, better quality, more durable roof would be seen as an improvement and be treated as a capital expenditure.

A third rule is whether the expenditure is considered to be for repair to an integral part of an existing asset or for a separate asset altogether. For example, the replacement of tires on a company vehicle would be considered an expense item, because even though the tires are themselves a separate asset, they form an integral part of the company vehicle. On the other hand, the cost of replacing a lathe in your workshop would be regarded as a capital expenditure because the lathe is not an integral part of the workshop.

The fourth rule concerns the relative value of the expenditure in comparison to the value of the whole property or to other repair and maintenance costs. The purchase of a spark plug for an engine is a separate asset, but no one would consider it anything other than an expense to maintain the engine. On the other hand, the purchase of an entirely new engine may be considered capital, given the significant cost of such a repair to the vehicle.

The fifth rule concerns repairs or installation costs for new and used property. If you purchase used equipment that requires repairs to make it suitable for use, then the repairs would be considered capital, even if the repairs would normally have been considered an expense. This is because the repairs are really considered a part of the purchase of the equipment. Similarly, the cost of installing equipment will be considered a part of the purchase of the equipment. For example, if you have to hire an electrician to hook up a new table saw, the cost of the hook-up would be considered part of the cost of the equipment.

The sixth and last rule concerns repairs made in anticipation of or as a condition of the sale of the property. Where this is the case, the repairs are normally considered a capital expenditure. On the other hand, if the repairs were going to be made in any event, and did not relate to the anticipated sale, the repairs would remain as an expense.

Once you have decided that an expenditure is capital, you must then decide how and if it can be deducted. There are three categories to consider. The first category is *non-deductible expenditures*. Land is a good example of this category, or assets you have purchased for your personal use only. You cannot deduct the cost of land or personal use items.

The second category is *depreciable property*. This is the most common category for capital purchases and would include computers, automobiles, and most other tangible assets that you would buy for your business.

The third category is *eligible capital expenditures*. These include the non-tangible assets like the incorporation costs. This category will be discussed in more detail later in this Round.

TAX BEATER

Maximize tax savings by knowing the difference between a capital and an expense purchase.

Included in the Appendix is a list of some of the more common capital expenditures for small and home-based businesses.

What Is Capital Cost Allowance (CCA)?

A common capital expenditure for small-business entrepreneurs is the purchase of depreciable property. Depreciable property purchased for business purposes can be deducted on your tax return, but not all at once. Instead of being able to deduct depreciable property immediately as an expense, you can only deduct these expenditures over time in the form of depreciation. The tax department calls this depreciation *capital cost allowance* or CCA.

To ensure that everyone depreciates similar assets at the same rate, the government has set the rates for depreciating certain assets. This is done by setting up different classes of assets. For example, the computer you purchased would be included in class 50 and can be depreciated at a rate of 55% per year. That bookcase would be a class 8 asset and can be depreciated at a rate of 20% per year. By establishing these classes and what assets go into each class, the government can ensure that no one gets an unfair advantage by depreciating assets too quickly and deferring tax. I have included in the Appendix a list of common asset purchases made by small and home-based businesses, their classes, and the rate of depreciation or CCA you can claim.

Are There Any Special Rules in the Year of Purchase?

TAX BEATER

Claim full depreciation on assets not subject to the half-rate rule.

Most capital assets that are purchased are eligible for only half the maximum capital cost allowance in the year of purchase. For example, if you purchased a piece of manufacturing equipment for $3,000, the equipment would qualify as a class 43 asset, which would mean that it can be depreciated at a maximum rate of 30% per year. However, in the year you purchased the equipment you can claim only half of the normal CCA. The next year, you will be able to claim the full 30% on the remaining balance.

It's important to note, though, that not all assets you purchase are subject to this half-rate rule. There are a handful of purchases that are exempt from this rule. The list of common asset purchases for small and home-based businesses included in the Appendix notes which assets are not subject to the half-rate rule. You can score a few points by ensuring you claim full CCA on these assets.

What Happens When I Sell an Asset?

When you sell a capital asset, you have to reduce the balance of the class to which the capital asset relates by the lesser of the original cost of the asset or the proceeds you received on the sale. For example, assume you sell that piece of manufacturing equipment you purchased for $3,000 to someone else for $2,000. You would reduce the value of class 43 by $2,000, representing the lesser of the purchase price, $3,000, and the proceeds you received, $2,000.

If there is a balance remaining in the class and there are other assets that belong to that class that you still own, the balance is just carried forward for future CCA claims.

If there is a positive balance remaining in the class and there are no other assets belonging to that class that you still own, you can deduct the remaining balance in the current year. This is referred to as claiming a *terminal loss*. For example, assume the only asset in class 43 is the equipment you bought for $3,000. In the first year we claimed CCA of $3,000 x 30% x 1/2 or $450. The 30% represents the maximum CCA rate for manufacturing equipment and the 1/2 represents the half-rate rule. The balance remaining in the class would be $2,550 or $3,000 minus the $450 CCA. If we then sold the machinery for $2,000, the balance remaining would be $550. If there were no other assets in class 43, the full $550 could be deducted in the current year to reduce income taxes.

TAX BEATER

Claim terminal losses to maximize your tax savings.

If there is a negative balance remaining in the class, the negative balance must be added to income, regardless of whether or not there are any assets remaining in the class. This is referred to as *recapture*. For example, assume that instead of selling the machinery in year two for $2,000, you sold it for $3,000. The balance in that class after the first year's CCA was $2,550. If you subtract $3,000 from that, you end up with a negative balance of $450. This must be added to your income in the current year.

Do I Have to Claim Full CCA?

Nowhere in the rules does it say that each year you have to claim full CCA. In fact, there are cases where you may not want to claim full CCA. Assume your business is losing money. Previous losses have already been used to obtain refunds in prior years. In this case it may make sense not to claim CCA. Save the deduction for future years.

TAX BEATER

Delay claiming CCA in times where you may lose the use of the deduction.

Remember the "Tax Rate Stairway," careful planning to maximize lower tax levels may involve deferring your CCA claim. However, care should be taken with this type of planning. If you don't claim CCA in one year, you cannot double up your CCA claim in the next year. You are always limited to the maximum rate for that class. Therefore, deferring CCA will just place you one year behind in depreciating the assets of that class.

TAX BEATER

When deferring CCA deductions, start by deferring fast-depreciating assets first to provide maximum flexibility.

For maximum flexibility and tax savings it is always wise, if you're considering deferring a CCA claim, to start by deferring the write-off of fast-depreciating assets first. For example, computer software is depreciated at the fast rate of 100%, but subject to the half-rate rule. Therefore, 50% is depreciated in the first year and 50% in the second year. If you defer claiming CCA on the computer software, you will be able to claim 100% of the CCA in the second or later year. This provides you with the maximum flexibility to manipulate your income, save tax dollars, and "Beat the Taxman."

Is There a Right Time of the Year to Purchase Assets?

In many cases, the needs of your business will dictate when it is necessary to purchase a particular asset. However, if you have sufficient flexibility to time the purchase of a capital asset to maximize your tax savings, the best time to purchase assets from an income tax point of view is at the end of the business year. If the year-end of your business is December, you can obtain maximum tax savings by purchasing the asset in December as opposed to January of the next year.

By purchasing the depreciable asset at the end of the business year, you are speeding up the claiming of the CCA. The amount of CCA will not change, but you can claim it more quickly. Assume you have a December year-end and you are contemplating purchasing some manufacturing equipment for $3,000. It is now December 2008, and you're debating whether to buy it before Christmas or after Christmas, in January of 2009. From an income tax point of view, purchasing the equipment in December will provide the maximum tax savings since in the current year you would be able to claim $450 in CCA ($3,000 x 30% x 1/2) and then, in the next year, you would be able to claim $765 in CCA ($3,000 – $450 = $2,550 x 30%). Despite the fact that you purchased the equipment in the last month of the year, you are still eligible to claim one-half of the year's CCA.

> **TAX BEATER**
>
> Purchase assets at the end of the business year instead of the beginning of the next year.

Alternatively, if you wait until January, 2009, to purchase the equipment, you would have to wait until December of 2009 to claim any CCA on the equipment. In that year you could claim $450 in CCA and then, not until the following year, or 2010, could you claim the $765 in CCA. By delaying the purchase by one month, you delay the timing of the tax savings by one full year.

In order to claim CCA on new purchases, it is important to ensure that the asset is available-for-use. Assuming your year-end is December, you can't pay for the equipment in December, 2008, and have it delivered in January, 2009, and still

TAX BEATER

Ensure that
your capital
purchase is
available-for-
use by the end
of your business
year, even if you
don't, in fact,
use it.

be able to claim CCA in December, 2009. Despite the fact that you have paid for the equipment, it is not available-for-use at your year-end since you didn't take possession of the equipment until January.

It is important to realize that there is a difference between available-for-use and use. Maybe you don't have a need for that equipment until February or March and you don't turn it on until then. You would still be eligible to claim CCA as long as you could have used the equipment in December. Available-for-use does not mean you actually have to use it.

Is There a Right Time to Sell Capital Assets?

As a general rule, from a tax point of view, it is best to defer the sale of assets until the beginning of your next business year. When you sell a capital asset, you reduce the balance of the class by the lesser of the original cost of the asset or the proceeds received on disposing of the asset. By reducing the balance in the class, you also reduce the amount of CCA you can claim in a year.

Assume that you are looking to sell the piece of manufacturing equipment, for proceeds of $2,000. Assume also that the balance in class 43 at the end of the year is $10,000, due to the purchase of other assets over the years. If you dispose of the equipment in December, your year-end, the maximum CCA you can claim is $2,400 ($10,000 – $2,000 x 30%). On the other hand, if you wait until January to sell that equipment, the maximum CCA for the current year would be $3,000 ($10,000 x 30%). By delaying the sale by one month, you have increased your tax deductions by $600, which could amount to a $276 tax savings.

TAX BEATER

Near your year-
end, delay the
sale of a capital
asset until early
the next year.

An observant reader would say that, yes, you get a greater deduction, but eventually it will catch up to you and you will have less of a CCA claim in a year due to this planning. And they would be right. But eventually could be a long time, depending on new purchases and other activities. And besides, as discussed previously, effective tax planning is deferring as long as possible the payment of tax. Even if the deferral is only for one year, it is better to pay tax next year than right now.

How Can I Save Tax Dollars with Capital Assets?

Not all capital purchases are treated equally. The faster an asset can be written off, the faster the tax savings can be realized on the purchase. The importance of properly identifying what class a capital asset belongs to and how it should be treated cannot be over-emphasized. Misclassifying capital additions can delay for years the tax savings you could otherwise have enjoyed. The following are some of the more common small and home-based business capital asset purchases that are treated uniquely.

Computer Software

Computer software that you purchase (other than system software, the internal software previously installed on your computer) is eligible to be written off at the fast rate of 100%, subject to the half-rate rule. Software is included in class 12. It is important to break out the software you purchase at the same time as the computer, and not include the whole purchase price as computer equipment, which is deductible at a lower rate.

TAX BEATER

When purchasing a computer and software at the same time, break out the software portion of the purchase and deduct at the 100% CCA rate.

Electronic Office Equipment

With electronic office equipment becoming outdated at increasingly rapid rates, there is a tendency to replace this equipment faster than it is depreciated. This can result in the unenviable position of depreciating assets you don't own. For example, consider the purchase of a $3,000 fax machine. After two years you decide that this machine is just not cutting it, so you purchase another machine and sell the old one for $200. The old machine would have depreciated only to $2,160 after two years of maximum CCA. Since you purchased a new machine which is added to the class, you would not normally be able to claim the loss in value from $2,160 to $200 in the current year. Instead, you would continue to claim CCA at 20% on the balance in the class 8 pool. This results in a slow depreciation of the old fax machine, which you don't own anymore.

To alleviate this problem, the government will allow you to place certain electronic office equipment into separate classes. The type of office equipment that will qualify for this treatment includes computer software, fax machines, photocopiers, and telephone equipment. How the system works is instead of adding the fax machine to all of the other equipment in class 8 you create a separate class 8 for each piece of electronic office equipment purchased. The CCA rate for the separate class will be the same as the normal class, but by placing the asset in a separate class, you can claim a terminal loss on the equipment if you sell it early at a loss. For example, assume the above fax machine purchase had been allocated to a separate class 8. The CCA rate is still 20% subject to the half-rate rule in the first year. But in year three, if the asset is sold for $200, then the loss of $1,960 ($2,160 balance remaining in the separate class 8 minus the $200 proceeds on the sale) would be fully deductible in the current year.

In order to take advantage of this rule, the capital asset must be purchased after April 26, 1993, must have cost more than $1,000, and you must elect to treat the addition in this manner when you file your tax return for the year you purchased the equipment. To elect to treat the addition in this manner, just attach a note to Canada Revenue Agency stating that you elect to include the electronic office equipment that you purchased in the current year in a separate class. If you still own the equipment after five years, the separate class must be added to the remaining pool.

TAX BEATER

Elect to include electronic office equipment in a separate CCA class to potentially increase your tax savings on sale.

Manufacturing and Processing Machinery and Equipment

In recognition that, like electronic office equipment, certain types of manufacturing and processing equipment become outdated quickly, the government announced in their 2000 budget that manufacturing and processing equipment that is included in Class 43 can be added in a separate class. Just like the special treatment for electronic office equipment, a separate class can be used for these additions provided that the equipment cost more than $1,000 and was acquired after February 27, 2000. To obtain this special tax treatment, a note must accompany your tax return in the year the asset is purchased stating that you elect to include the manufacturing and processing machinery and equipment in a separate class. As well, if you still own the equipment after five years, the separate class must be added to the remaining Class 43 pool.

> **TAX BEATER**
>
> Elect to include manufacturing and processing machinery and equipment in a separate CCA class to potentially increase your tax savings on sale.

Small Tools

Small tools that cost less than $500 are treated as class 12 asset additions not subject to the half-rate rule. This means that small tools costing less than $500 each can be fully expensed in the current year. If a tool costs more than $500, unless it falls under a different class, it will need to be added to class 8 and depreciated at 20% per year.

> **TAX BEATER**
>
> Deduct 100% of the cost of tools costing less than $500.

Remember, this rule is looked at on an individual tool-by-tool basis. If you purchase more than one tool, the invoice may be greater than $500. However, as long as the individual tools are less than $500 each, they should qualify for the 100% write-off.

Can I Deduct the Cost of a Personal Asset That Is Now Being Used in the Business?

> **TAX BEATER**
>
> Deduct CCA on personal assets which are now being used in your business.

If you start using a personal capital asset in your business, you can deduct capital cost allowance on that capital asset. When you begin using a personal asset in the business, there is a deemed change in use of that asset. It no longer is considered a personal asset, but is instead considered a business asset.

As a result of the change in use, you are considered to have sold the asset to your business. Even though no cash will trade hands, you are treated as if the "personal you" sold it to the "business you." In most cases, the value you place on the asset will be its fair market value at the time of the change in use. In other words, the value you would use as an addition to the CCA schedule is the value you would pay if you were purchasing the same asset from a stranger.

For example, assume you have just started the business and the business is going to use your personal computer. The cost of the computer was $3,000, but today it is worth only $1,000. You would add $1,000 to class 50 for the value of the computer. The difference between $3,000 and $1,000 is not deductible, since this decrease in value occurred while the computer was owned by you personally.

If you change the use of an asset that has gone up in value, the calculation can be somewhat more complicated. Your starting point is the same, that is, estimating the fair market value of the asset. However, you must deduct from that any capital gains exemption claimed on that property, but only to the point that it may reduce the fair market value down to the original cost. In addition, you may have to report a capital gain on the transfer of the property.

For example, assume that you are going to turn your cottage into a fishing store and boat rental office. On your 1994 income tax return, you used the capital gains exemption on that cottage in the amount of $20,000 ($7,000 related to the land and $13,000 related to the building). The land originally cost $10,000 and the building $50,000. The value of the cottage is now estimated at $100,000 (land value $20,000 and building value $80,000). The amount that you could add to your CCA building class would be $67,000, that is, $80,000 minus the capital gains exemption on the building of $13,000.

You will also have to report a capital gain on this change in use of the cottage. Since you are considered to have sold your cottage at its fair market value when you turn it into a business property, you will have to pay tax on any increase in value in the property. In this case, the capital gain on the total property would be $20,000. See the following chart for details on how this is calculated.

Calculation of Capital Gain	Building	Land	Total
	$	$	$
Cost	50	10	60
Elected capital gain	13	7	20
	63	17	80
Fair Market Value Now	80	20	100
Capital Gain	17	3	20
Calculation of Addition to CCA Class			
Fair Market Value	80	* N/A	80
Less Elected Capital Gain	13	N/A	13
Eligible Addition to CCA claim	67	N/A	67

* Cannot claim CCA on land

Can I Claim CCA on Assets Used Only Part of the Time in My Business?

When assets are used part of the time in your business and part of the time personally, you can still claim CCA on the asset. However, you are restricted in how much you can claim, based on a reasonable estimate of how long the asset was used for business purposes. For example, assume the computer is used part of the time in the business and it is also used by the kids for homework and video games. And let's say you estimate that the business use is about 60% of the total time the computer is being used. To calculate how much CCA can be claimed in the business, first calculate the maximum amount of CCA that can be claimed on the computer. At 55%, this would be $825 in the first year, remembering the 1/2 rate rule

TAX BEATER

Deduct a portion of the cost of assets used both personally and in a business.

for the first year. Multiply that by 60%. The remaining 40% is not tax deductible.

Should I Claim CCA on My Personal Residence?

In most cases your tax coach would not recommend claiming CCA on your house for the single reason that when you go to sell your home, you may find yourself paying some tax. Normally when you sell your home, you don't have to pay any tax on the increase in value of the home because of an exemption called the "principal residence exemption." If you convert 10% of your home into an office and you claim 10% of the CCA available on the cost of your home, then when you go to sell, 10% of any increase in value will be taxable as a capital gain. In addition, when you do sell your home, you will have to include in your income, and pay tax on, the CCA that you had claimed over the years. In most cases the tax deduction is just not worth the extra tax you may have to pay.

Claiming CCA may make sense where you have more than one personal residence, like a cottage, and you were not planning to use the principal residence exemption on your home that has the office. Or, you are really sure that your home will not be sold at a profit.

What Is an Eligible Capital Expenditure?

An eligible capital expenditure is a type of expenditure that doesn't really fit as a depreciable expenditure, nor can it be reasonably expensed in the current year. Eligible capital expenditures are often referred to as "nothings" or "intangibles" because the expenditure is for something that can't be seen or felt. A good example is goodwill you purchase when buying an existing business. The goodwill typically represents the positive name of the business in the community, good employee morale, excellent customer relations, and so on. It is often because of the goodwill built up in a business that you are willing to pay more for it. Another example of an eligible capital expenditure is the cost of an unlimited life franchise or licence. These expenditures are certainly valuable, but you can't point to them and say here is what I purchased.

Another common eligible capital expenditure is legal and accounting fees spent to incorporate a business. Canada Revenue Agency considers these expenses to have a long-term benefit; therefore, they are not a current expense. On the other hand, there is no CCA class that could handle professional fees spent to incorporate a business. Accordingly, these fees fall into the category of eligible capital expenditures.

Can I Deduct Eligible Capital Expenditures?

You can deduct eligible capital expenditures, but like depreciable expenditures, you can deduct them only over time.

However, unlike depreciable expenditures, you can deduct only three-quarters of an eligible capital expenditure.

Three-quarters of all eligible capital expenditures that you purchase for your business are added to one pool. Each year you can deduct 7% of the balance in that pool. As you can see, it will take a long time to deduct an eligible capital expenditure.

Can I Deduct My Own Goodwill?

I am often asked: If goodwill is an eligible capital expenditure, can I deduct the goodwill that I have created in my business? Unfortunately, the answer to this is no. You can deduct only the goodwill that you have purchased from someone else.

Am I Taxed on the Goodwill I Sell?

When you sell your business, if a portion of the purchase price is allocated to goodwill, then you may be taxed on the sale of that goodwill. If your year-end is after October 17, 2000, then one-half of the proceeds you receive on the sale of goodwill will be deducted from the cumulative eligible capital (CEC) pool. If no other eligible capital expenditures have been added to the CEC pool, then one-half of the proceeds from the sale of your goodwill will be subject to tax.

If there have been additions to your CEC pool over the years, then the calculation of how much of the proceeds that must be treated as income is a lot more complicated. The basic concept however, is that you must first add to income the amount of amortization you have claimed in the past for your eligible capital expenditures and compare this to your proceeds from the sale of your goodwill. You must be careful however, that you take into consideration the different inclusion rates used over the past number of years for your addition. Then any excess will be included in income as discussed above.

The calculation of taxable income from the sale of goodwill is very complex. If done correctly, you can save considerable tax dollars due to the beneficial tax treatment given to eligible capital expenditures. However, if calculated incorrectly, you can lose this round. If you are selling goodwill, seek out a good tax coach to help you.

AUTO-matic Savings

Most entrepreneurs want to deduct the costs of operating an automobile used in their business. And rightly so. Deducting automobile costs is very important in reducing your tax liability. It is one of the tax deductions that I am frequently asked about and ranks right up there with home-office expenses in importance. It is also, unfortunately, one of the more complex areas for small businesses, with many rules and restrictions. However, knowing these rules and planning your affairs accordingly can provide you with significant tax savings and will ensure that you win Round 10.

What Automobile Expenses Can I Deduct?

As a general rule, you can deduct any expense incurred to operate your vehicle. This includes the gas and oil to run the vehicle, the maintenance and repairs to keep the vehicle on the road, the licence and registration fees, the insurance costs, leasing costs or capital cost allowance, and interest costs if you borrowed to purchase the vehicle.

If you use your vehicle strictly for business purposes, you will be eligible to deduct 100% of the motor vehicle expenses. However, in many cases the vehicle is used for both business and personal use. In this case, you are eligible to deduct only those automobile expenses that relate to the business. To determine how much of an expense is eligible to be deducted, divide your total business kilometres in a year by the total kilometres driven and multiply this by your automobile expenses.

For example, assume that your automobile expenses amounted to $3,000 in the year and your business kilometres equalled 15,000 kilometres. Your total annual driving was 20,000 kilometres. The amount you can deduct on your tax return for automobile expenses would be:

$$\$3,000 \quad \times \quad \frac{15,000 \text{ (business kilometres)}}{20,000 \text{ (total kilometres)}} \quad = \quad \$2,250$$

To ensure that you can obtain the maximum tax deduction for your vehicle, make sure you keep all receipts to support your automobile expenses and that you keep some sort of log or record of your business kilometres. Remember, if you are challenged on your tax deductions, it is up to you to prove that your deduction is reasonable.

TAX BEATER

Record all business kilometres you drive.

Canada Revenue Agency suggests that you keep a log for all of your business trips, which includes the date of the trip, destination, purpose, and number of kilometres driven. Unfortunately, not everyone is disciplined enough to keep such a log. What happens is that you forget business kilometres and don't claim them, or the tax auditor reduces your claim since there is no support for the business kilometres.

TAX BEATER

Keep all automotive receipts to support your tax deduction.

If keeping a log is not for you, consider this trick. If you carry an appointment book around with you, write down beside the appointment the number of kilometres driven. Include in your appointment book business errands you have to run and write the kilometres driven for those. At the end of the month add up the kilometres driven and write that down in the back of the book. With this method you have the date and approximate time the driving occurred, you have the kilometres driven, you have the customer name, and possibly the purpose of the trip. You will have all the information needed without having to keep separate logs.

Remember that you can have more than one personal vehicle that is used in your business. If you use two or more vehicles interchangeably, keep track of all auto expenses for both vehicles and then divide the number of business kilometres by the total kilometres for both vehicles to arrive at the amount of automotive expenses that can be deducted.

If you have two personal vehicles at home and you need only one, you may want to consider using the vehicle with the most operating costs in the business. If one vehicle is paid for and does not require any maintenance, whereas the other vehicle still has a loan outstanding, requires more maintenance, and is less fuel efficient, you can increase your tax deductions by using the second vehicle in your business. This especially makes sense if both vehicles are being driven about the same number of kilometres per year.

At the year-end of your business, remember to record the odometer reading on the vehicles you are using in your business. If this is your first year of operation or if you are just beginning to claim auto expenses, remember to record the odometer reading at the beginning of your business year or from the point that you are beginning to use the vehicle in the business.

The odometer reading is important to calculate the overall kilometres driven in your business's fiscal year. If you estimate this number, you may estimate too high, which will reduce the amount of auto expenses you can claim as a tax deduction.

As a self-employed owner of a business, you are not allowed to simply take a per kilometre charge and deduct this as an auto expense. You must keep your receipts relating to your automobile and deduct the actual costs. The per kilometre

TAX BEATER

If two or more vehicles are used in your business, keep track of the business kilometres on each vehicle to maximize your tax deductions.

TAX BEATER

Maximize tax savings by using the vehicle with higher operating costs.

TAX BEATER

Record your odometer readings at the beginning and end of each year.

allowance is reserved for your employees if you reimburse them for auto expenses incurred on business. As an owner of your sole proprietorship, you cannot be considered an employee and would therefore not be eligible for a per-kilometre allowance.

What Is Considered "Business Travel"?

Travelling on business includes any reasonable travelling you conduct to and from your customer's place of business or in the performance of your business. This includes travelling to the store or to a different city to purchase business supplies, travelling to meet a client to conduct business, or travelling to and from a business conference or course.

TAX BEATER

Schedule client meetings on the way to and from work to increase business kilometres and save taxes.

However, if you have an office away from your home, travelling to and from your office would not be considered business travelling. This is personal. On the other hand, if your office is at home and a client provides you an office on a temporary basis to conduct business, travelling back and forth to that office would usually be considered business travelling.

If you do have an office away from your home, a legitimate way to increase your business kilometres is to schedule meetings with clients on the way to and from work. This will turn a non-deductible personal trip into a fully deductible business trip.

Can I Deduct the Cost of My Car in the Business?

As I have already stated, you can deduct the cost of your vehicle in the business, subject to certain restrictions, provided it is used for business purposes. However, a vehicle is considered a capital asset and therefore can only be deducted over time in the form of capital cost allowance (CCA). (See Round 9 for more details on capital assets.) As well, you can deduct only the portion of the capital cost allowance that relates to business use. Follow the same rules to calculate what the maximum capital cost allowance would be for the year by multiplying the CCA amount by the number of business kilometres over the total kilometres driven, but beware, there are special rules (I warned you this was a complex area!).

If the vehicle was purchased after December 31, 2000, and cost less than $30,000, then there would be no other restrictions beyond that stated in the previous paragraph. The vehicle would be considered a class 10 asset and eligible for a 30% CCA rate, subject to the half-rate rule in the year of purchase.

If the cost of the vehicle is greater than $30,000 before GST and any provincial sales tax, as applicable, then an additional restriction may apply to reduce the amount of CCA that may be claimed. If the vehicle is considered to be a passenger vehicle, you will be restricted in how much of the cost of the vehicle you can deduct in your business.

The intention of the legislation is to reduce the amount that could be deducted in a business on expensive luxury vehicles. The government has set a threshold of $30,000 plus GST and PST on purchases of vehicles after December 31, 2000. If you purchase a passenger vehicle that costs more than $30,000, you will only be able to add $30,000 plus the applicable GST and PST on $30,000 to your CCA schedule. If you are eligible to claim GST input tax credits you will not be able to add the GST to your CCA schedule, unless you are a sole proprietor or in a partnership and you use the vehicle less than 90% of the time for business purposes. (See Round 6 for more details on how the GST refund works.)

These restrictions have been around since they were first introduced on June 17, 1987. However, the threshold level has changed over the years.

In fact, every year, usually in December, the government reviews these threshold levels and other auto rates and limits and announces any changes for the upcoming year. The rates and limits found on the following pages are the current rates as we went to press. You may wish to contact your Canada Revenue Agency office if you require rates and limits in effect after December 31, 2008.

The following chart shows a history of the CCA restriction on passenger vehicles over the years.

HISTORY OF THE CCA RESTRICTION

Time Frame	Restriction
On June 17, 1987, and before Sept 1, 1989	$20,000
On Sept 1, 1989, and before Jan 1, 1991	$24,000
On Jan 1, 1991, and before Jan 1, 1997	$24,000 plus PST and GST payable on $24,000
On Jan 1, 1997, and before Jan 1, 1998	$25,000 plus PST and GST payable on $25,000
On Jan 1, 1998, and before Jan 1, 2000	$26,000 plus PST and GST payable on $26,000
On Jan 1, 2000, and before Jan 1, 2001	$27,000 plus PST and GST payable on $27,000
On and after Jan 1, 2001	$30,000 plus PST and GST payable on $30,000

With class 10.1 come some peculiar tax treatments. For example, only one vehicle is added to each 10.1 class. Therefore, if you have two passenger vehicles you are using in your business that exceed the $30,000 threshold, you will have two class 10.1 entries on your CCA schedule.

If you sell a class 10.1 vehicle, despite the fact that there is only one asset in the class, you will not be allowed to claim a *terminal loss* or be required to include *recapture* in your income. In Round 9 I showed how, when the last asset of a class was sold, you could claim a terminal loss or recapture on your tax return. However, with class 10.1 assets, no terminal loss or recapture is allowed. Instead, you can claim one-half of the normal CCA you would have been able to claim on the vehicle had you still owned it at the year-end. The balance remaining in the class 10.1 pool just disappears.

With a class 10.1 vehicle, the cost of the vehicle that is in excess of the $30,000 threshold never gets deducted for tax purposes. This is obviously not a desirable result. Where possible, you should take steps to reduce the effect of this limitation.

One way to maximize your tax deductions is to review what types of vehicles are considered passenger vehicles and what types are not. For example, a minivan that is used more than 50% of the time to transport goods and equipment, and that cannot accommodate more than the driver and two passengers, would not be considered a passenger vehicle. Therefore, even if the minivan cost $40,000, it would be an eligible class 10 asset and depreciated in the business subject to the normal business use restrictions. On the other hand, a minivan that can accommodate more than three passengers would be considered a passenger vehicle, unless it is used to transport goods, equipment or passengers for more than 90% of the time in the business. The "Vehicle Definition" chart on the next page may be helpful for deciding which class your vehicle belongs to.

> **TAX BEATER**
>
> Maximize your tax savings by purchasing vehicles that are not considered passenger vehicles.

Another way to maximize your tax deductions is by negotiating a good deal on your vehicle purchase. If you can negotiate a lower price for your vehicle by possibly accepting less on your trade-in, you might be able to avoid the class 10.1 treatment. For example, let's say you are considering purchasing a $31,000 vehicle which would normally be considered a passenger vehicle and you are trading in a vehicle which may be worth $13,000. The dealership is going to receive $18,000 cash after the trade-in. So if you could negotiate a purchase price of only $29,000 for the new vehicle and accept, say, $11,000 for the trade-in, then you could avoid the class 10.1

VEHICLE DEFINITIONS

Type of Vehicle	Seating (includes driver)	Business use in year bought or leased	Vehicle definition
Coupe, sedan, station wagon, sports or luxury car	1 to 9	1% to 100%	passenger
Pick-up truck used to transport goods or equipment	1 to 3	more than 50%	motor
Pick-up truck (other than above)	1 to 3	1% to 100%	passenger
Pick-up truck with extended cab used to transport goods, equipment or passengers	4 to 9	90% or more	motor
Pick-up truck with extended cab used to transport goods, equipment or passengers to a remote work site	4 to 9	50% or more	motor
Pick-up truck with extended cab (other than above)	4 to 9	1% to 100%	passenger
Sport utility used to transport goods, equipment or passengers	4 to 9	90% or more	motor
Sport utility (other than above)	4 to 9	1% to 100%	passenger
Van or minivan used to transport goods or equipment	1 to 3	more than 50%	motor
Van or minivan (other than above)	1 to 3	1% to 100%	passenger
Van or minivan used to transport goods, equipment or passengers	4 to 9	90% or more	motor
Van or minivan (other than above)	4 to 9	1% to 100%	passenger

Source: Canada Revenue Agency

restrictions. Since the dealership will still get their $18,000 cash, they may be willing to help you out.

Of course, the tax department could argue that the trade-in value was too low and adjust the deal. However, by having the invoice structured in your favour at the beginning, it will provide you with the support to make the claim. Also, the transaction is between two parties operating as strangers to each other. In all but the most obviously aggressive situations, the invoice will likely stand and you will be able to avoid the class 10.1 restrictions.

> **TAX BEATER**
> Avoid class 10.1 restrictions by negotiating favourable new vehicle purchase deals.

Are There Any Restrictions on Lease Costs?

Yes. You can't get around the class 10.1 restrictions by leasing a vehicle instead. Similar restrictions are in place to limit on an annual basis the amount of lease costs which may be deducted in your business. The lease restriction rules are very complex. Their intent is to equalize the benefits to an individual who purchases a vehicle and an individual who leases a vehicle.

Generally, the lease restriction is calculated as the lesser of two calculations. The first calculation is as follows:

$$\frac{\$800 \text{ (plus GST and PST as applicable)} \times \text{\# of days the vehicle was leased from the beginning of the lease}}{30} - \begin{array}{c}\text{lease payments}\\\text{deducted in}\\\text{prior years}\end{array}$$

The second calculation is:

$$\frac{\$30,000 \text{ (plus GST and PST as applicable)} \times \text{actual lease charges in the year}}{.85 \times \text{greater of i) manufacturer's list price plus the PST that would be charged}}$$

or
ii) $35,295 plus GST and PST on $35,295 as applicable

You are allowed to deduct the lesser of these two calculations. These formulas are based on a lease that was started after January 1, 2001. If the lease began before January 1, 2001, and on or after January 1, 2000, then the lease restriction is calculated using the same formula but with the following prescribed amounts: in the first calculation, the lease payment limit is $700 instead of $800; in the second calculation replace $30,000 with $27,000 in the numerator and replace $35,295 with $31,765 in the denominator. If the lease began before January 1, 2000 and on or after January 1, 1998, then the lease restriction is calculated using the following prescribed amounts: in the first calculation the lease payment limit is $650; in the second calculation, use $26,000 in the numerator and $30,588 in the denominator. If the lease began before January 1, 1998 and on or after January 1, 1997, then the lease restriction is calculated using the following prescribed amounts: in the first calculation the lease payment limit is $550; in the second calculation, use $25,000 in the numerator and $29,412 in the denominator. If the lease began before January 1, 1997, and on or after January 1, 1991, then the lease restriction is calculated using the following prescribed amounts: in the first calculation the lease payment limit is $650; in the second calculation, use $24,000 in the numerator and $28,235 in the denominator.

If the lease began before January 1, 1991, you should contact Canada Revenue Agency for the previous prescribed amounts. In addition, these formulas will become more complex if you make a refundable deposit on the lease and if you receive reimbursements.

TAX BEATER

Maximize your lease deduction by keeping operating expenses out of the lease agreement.

Generally speaking, if your lease costs are less than $800 per month, then you should not fall into the above restrictions. One way to ensure that your lease costs are kept low is to structure your lease agreement to exclude insurance, repairs, maintenance, and licences. If these costs are included, consider requesting that they be valued and broken out of the agreement. Where these costs are included in the lease payments, you must include the costs in the above restrictions.

Can I Deduct All Interest Charges on My Vehicle?

You can deduct interest paid to finance the purchase of a vehicle to the extent that the vehicle is used for business purposes. However, if the vehicle is considered a passenger vehicle, you will be limited to claiming up to a maximum of $300.00 per month interest on the vehicle if purchased after December 31, 2000. (On vehicles purchased after December 31, 1996 and before January 1, 2001 you can claim up to a maximum of $250.00 per month.

On vehicles purchased prior to 1997, you can claim up to a maximum of $300 per month.) At the end of the year, you can claim the lesser of the actual interest paid or $10.00 per day times the number of days that interest was paid. The lesser of these two numbers will still be restricted by the pro-ration of business use over total use.

TAX BEATER

Arrange new car financing so that none of the interest is restricted.

When borrowing money to purchase a passenger vehicle, it is wise to keep this interest restriction in mind. If you can arrange your affairs so that the interest will not exceed the maximum by using excess cash to finance the balance of the purchase price, you will maximize your tax savings.

Should I Own My Passenger Vehicle in My Corporation?

A frequently asked question is whether to own your car personally or in the corporation. There are several schools of thought on this and ultimately the decision will depend on your individual situation. However, if you like things simple, my advice is to own the car personally.

Over the years, the government has worked hard to remove the benefit of having personal use vehicles owned by a corporation. The corporation is subject to the same restrictions on capital cost allowance and lease costs as an individual. In addition, you will need to calculate and add to your T4 a taxable benefit referred to as a *standby charge* for the use of that vehicle.

The standby charge can be a very significant cost. Unless you are eligible for a standby charge reduction, the standby charge is calculated at a rate of 2% times the original cost of the vehicle (excluding GST, but including provincial sales tax) for each month the vehicle was available for your use. Note that the original cost is not limited by the $30,000 threshold amount. Therefore, your company may only be able to deduct $30,000 plus GST and PST as applicable, yet you will be assessed a standby charge on the full original value of the vehicle.

If the vehicle is leased, the standby charge is equal to two thirds of the lease cost of the vehicle, including any maintenance and repair costs included in the lease, but not including insurance. As is the case when the company owns the vehicle, the lease standby charge is calculated on the full lease cost, not the restricted amount allowed as a deduction to the company.

In addition, if the company pays all of the operating costs on the vehicle, i.e., gas, oil, maintenance and repairs, insurance, etc., you will also have to add to your T4 a taxable benefit for these operating expenses. This taxable benefit is calculated by multiplying 24 cents by the number of personal kilometres in the year. If your business is principally the selling or leasing of automobiles then the benefit is 21 cents times the number of personal kilometres in the year. If the vehicle is used at least 50% of the time for business purposes, you have the option of including 50% of the standby charge as a taxable benefit.

Prior to the February 2003 Federal Budget, if the vehicle was used 90% of the time or more in the business and your personal use was less than 1,000 kilometres per month, the standby charge was reduced by way of the following equation:

$$\frac{\text{Standby charge otherwise calculated} \times \text{Kilometres for personal use in the year}}{1,000 \times \text{number of months in the year in which the car was available}}$$

For example, if your personal kilometres averaged out to 100 kilometres per month and the vehicle was used at least 90% of the time for business use, you would only have to include 10% (1,200 km/12,000) of the standby charge in your income. This reduction applies equally whether the vehicle is leased or purchased.

The February 2003 budget changed the rules on how to calculate the standby charge reduction, making the rules more favourable for the taxpayer. The problem with the way the standby charge was calculated before was that it was often difficult to meet the 90% business use of the vehicle. And if you could not meet the 90% test, then you would not be eligible for the reduction. So the budget changed the rules to allow the reduced standby charge to apply if annual personal driving does not exceed 20,000 kilometres and the automobile is used primarily or more than 50% of the time for business purposes. This change in the rules will allow many more employees to be eligible for the reduced standby charge calculation. Now, provided that your business use is at least 50% of the total kilometres in a year, the reduced standby charge formulae will be as follows:

$$\text{Standby charge otherwise calculated} \times \frac{\text{Kilometres for personal use in the year}}{1{,}667 \times \text{number of months in the year in which the car was available}}$$

If you meet the conditions to allow for a reduced standby charge and consider it likely that you will continue to meet the conditions in the future, then it may be worthwhile to consider owning your vehicle within the company. It is a mathematical exercise to know if it is better to own your vehicle personally or within your company. Here is another example of where a good tax coach can help you win in the tax savings fight.

> **TAX BEATER**
> Consider whether to own your personal vehicle personally instead of in a corporation.

How Can I Reduce the Amount of the Standby Charge?

If your vehicle is in the company and you don't want to change this structure, you may be able to take some action to reduce the standby charge.

If your personal kilometres are relatively low, consider calculating your operating expense taxable benefit using the 24 cents per personal kilometre method rather than the easier method of just taking 50% of the standby charge. This will mean that you will have to keep track of your business or personal kilometres, but it may save you tax dollars over the long run.

Another way to reduce your standby charge is to keep track of when the vehicle is not available for your use. For example, keep track of when you're out of town and you don't have access to your car. If you take another family vehicle on vacations, exclude that time in the calculation of standby charge.

Another way you might reduce the standby charge is to compare the charge for a leased and purchased vehicle. You may find that including two thirds of the lease costs will be less expensive than 24% of the purchase cost.

One last trick to "Beat the Taxman" is to consider selling your vehicle to another one of your companies. If you have more than one operating company, consider selling the used vehicle to one of your other companies at its true fair market value. Remember, the standby charge is calculated at the rate of 2% per month times the original cost of the vehicle. If that vehicle cost you $50,000 five years ago, you will still be calculating a standby charge based on $50,000. It may only be worth $20,000 now. If that's the case, sell the vehicle to one of your other companies for $20,000. The standby charge will then be calculated at the lower purchase price.

A word of caution. The other company should be earning income of a type that would substantiate a vehicle expense. Otherwise, operating expenses and capital cost allowance would be denied in that company because they were not

---

TAX BEATER

When personal kilometres are low, use the 24 cents per personal kilometre method of calculating your operating taxable benefit.

TAX BEATER

Before purchasing your vehicle, compare the standby charge under the lease option.

TAX BEATER

Reduce your standby charge by selling your vehicle to one of your other operating companies.

incurred for the purpose of earning income. As well, depending on your province, you may have to pay provincial sales tax on the transfer of the vehicle.

If I Own My Car Personally How Should the Company Reimburse Me for Business Travelling?

If you have decided to own your car personally, but you use the vehicle for business travel, your corporation can reimburse you. You can structure this two ways. You can provide expense reports to the company on a periodic basis, detailing the business kilometres travelled, and receive a reasonable reimbursement on a per-kilometre basis. Alternatively, you can receive a reasonable tax-free allowance for business travel.

Canada Revenue Agency views a reasonable reimbursement on a per-kilometre basis to be equal to 52 cents per kilometre for the first 5,000 kilometres and 46 cents per kilometre thereafter. (Note that an additional 4 cents per kilometre is allowed if travelling in the Yukon, Northwest Territories, and Nunavut.) A reasonable allowance is viewed by Canada Revenue Agency as an allowance that is based on a per-business-kilometre rate and you are not receiving any other reimbursements for business travelling.

If the allowance or reimbursement is considered reasonable, then the allowance will not be taxable in your hands. If the allowance is based on a per-kilometre charge and you do not receive any other reimbursements, but Canada Revenue Agency considers the allowance to be unreasonably high, the allowance will be treated as a taxable benefit.

If the allowance is not based on a per-kilometre charge or you receive other reimbursements, the full allowance will be included in your income. However, you will then be allowed to deduct from that the actual costs to operate your vehicle for business purposes.

To ensure that your monthly car allowance is reasonable and therefore non-taxable to you, make sure the following

TAX BEATER

Save time and money: pay yourself a reasonable tax-free car allowance on personally owned vehicles.

three criteria are met, and then you should have no problems
with the Canada Revenue Agency:

- You have an employment contract and it states that the
  employee is to receive a certain amount for each business kilometre driven during the year;

- At year-end, compare the actual number of business
  kilometres driven with the advances received and the
  difference should either be paid to or collected from
  the employee; and

- Ensure that the set periodic amount advanced, the
  per-kilometre rate used, and the projected number of
  business kilometres to be driven in the year are all reasonable.

Saving by Spending

The government, from time to time, attempts to stimulate the economy or a particular segment of the economy by offering various incentive programs. Past programs that are no longer available include the New Hires Program and the Federal Youth Hires Program that encouraged employers to hire new employees or employees in a specific age group. The programs provided incentives through reduced EI premiums. A program that is still used by the government is the investment tax credit system. This program has been around for a long time and is still used by the government to provide incentives to various businesses and industries that invest in machinery equipment in certain areas of the country, create child care spaces or invest in Scientific Research and Experimental Development.

Different governments tend to have different philosophies about which part of the economy needs to be stimulated or how to go about it. As a result, some programs are only available for a short period of time and some programs go in and out of fashion. However, there are a couple of lucrative programs still around and you may be eligible to apply for past programs giving you that one-two combination to win this Round.

What Is an Investment Tax Credit?

Investment tax credits provide a reduction in your tax liability based on a set percentage of qualified purchases. For example, if you purchased some equipment for $200 that qualified for an ITC rebate of 20%, you could reduce the amount of tax you pay to the government by $40.

Most ITCs relate to the purchase of manufacturing and processing equipment, fishing and farming equipment, certain types of transportation and construction equipment, and research and development expenditures. If your business purchases do not fall into these categories, it is very likely that you will not be eligible for an investment tax credit. Since governments are trying to encourage specific industries and activities, ITCs are not for everyone.

TAX BEATER

Reduce the tax you pay with investment tax credits.

Who Can Claim Investment Tax Credits?

Investment tax credits can be claimed by individuals, partners in a partnership, or corporations. In order to claim investment tax credits you must be engaged in an activity or purchasing equipment in an area that will allow you the credit. For example, anyone who is involved in Scientific Research and Experimental Development (SR&ED) anywhere in Canada is eligible to claim an investment tax credit on their expenditures. As well, anyone who lives in the Atlantic provinces or the Gaspé Peninsula region of Quebec may be eligible for an investment tax credit on certain capital purchases made for their businesses.

In order to qualify for the investment tax credit in the maritime provinces or the Gaspé Peninsula region of Quebec (other than under the SR&ED program), the asset purchased must be new, and used in Canada primarily in an activity prescribed by the government, such as manufacturing or processing goods for sale or lease, farming, fishing, logging, storing grain, and producing industrial minerals.

Deciding what purchases qualify for investment tax credits is not an easy task. So if you feel you may have purchased some assets that would qualify for an investment tax credit, discuss it with your tax coach or contact Canada Revenue Agency. The potential tax savings is worth the time.

How Do I Claim an Investment Tax Credit?

If you are eligible to claim an investment tax credit for a purchase other than for scientific research and experimental development, all you will need to do is complete Form T2038 (IND), "Investment Tax Credit (Individuals)" and submit it with your completed tax return. With this form you will be able to calculate the amount of tax credit available by multiplying the cost of the purchase by the investment tax credit rate. You may then deduct this investment tax credit from taxes you would otherwise have to pay.

TAX BEATER

Apply for 40% investment tax credit refund to speed up tax savings.

If after deducting the eligible investment tax credit from your tax liability, there is still a balance left over, you may apply to have up to 40% of the balance refunded in the current year. Most investment tax credit programs offer this refundable feature.

If there is still a balance left over, the balance can be carried back three years to reduce tax liabilities, or forward ten years. This system should provide ample opportunity to make use of the investment tax credits. As a planning point, if it appears that investment tax credits may start to be lost, you should consider reducing discretionary expenses like not claiming CCA or not providing for receivables.

TAX BEATER

Apply unused investment tax credits to past and future taxation years.

Note that the request to have an investment tax credit applied to a previous year must be made with the filing of your tax return in the year the investment tax credit arose. If your tax return is filed late that year, Canada Revenue Agency has the authority not to accept the tax credit carry back. In most cases they will agree to carry the tax credit back, but if you file

TAX BEATER

Reduce CCA claims to use up investment tax credits before they expire.

TAX BEATER

File your tax return on time to ensure ITC carry backs are accepted by Canada Revenue Agency.

your tax return late, you run the risk of their saying no. It is another example of the importance of filing your tax return on time, even if you know you don't have a tax liability.

Investment tax credits are provided by the government as an incentive for you to make certain purchases. In effect, they are providing a rebate. Accordingly, that purchase didn't really cost you as much as you reported when you added it to the capital cost allowance schedule.

Recognizing this, the government requires you to reduce the balance in the capital cost allowance class by the amount of the investment tax credit refund you receive. You make the adjustment in the year after the year in which you reduce your income taxes. For example, say you purchase a $1,000 piece of equipment for manufacturing that is eligible for a 10% or $100 investment tax credit. When you purchased the equipment you would have added $1,000 to class 43, representing the cost of that equipment for that year. You applied for and will receive a refund of $100 as an investment tax credit. This $100 must be recorded as a reduction in class 43 next year. It will therefore reduce the amount of CCA claim that will be available in that year and future years.

What Expenditures Qualify for SR&ED?

One of the most lucrative incentive programs currently being offered in Canada is the Scientific Research and Experimental Development (SR&ED) program. To qualify under this program you must be engaged in an activity that qualifies as scientific research and experimental development. The Income Tax Act defines SR&ED as "a systematic investigation or search carried out in a field of science or technology by means of experiment or analysis." SR&ED includes:

- basic research that is engaged in just to further scientific knowledge, even though there may be no specific application of this knowledge

- applied research, which is research engaged to further scientific knowledge with a specific application in mind

- experimental development, which is work undertaken to achieve technological advancement for the purpose of creating something new or significantly improved.

So, basically, SR&ED includes research for the sake of research, research with a specific use in mind, and the development of a new and improved product. However, in order for an expenditure to qualify as SR&ED, the expenditure must be related to a business you are engaged in, the expenditure must be in the scientific or technology field, there must be some sort of technological or scientific advancement and up until February 28, 2008, the activity must happen in Canada. As a result of the 2008 budget, claimants can earn SR&ED investment tax credits on certain salaries or wages for SR&ED work performed outside Canada after February 25, 2008. However, in order for the salaries and wages you incur outside of Canada to qualify, the SR&ED work performed outside of the country must be directly undertaken by your employees and the work that they perform must form part of the SR&ED you are undertaking in Canada. Eligible salaries or wages in a tax year will be limited to 10 percent of the total of salary or wages for SR&ED performed in Canada.

Normally, in order to qualify there must be some uncertainty about the outcome of the work that you are doing. If you know what you are creating will work, then you are not likely engaged in SR&ED.

Keep in mind also, that it is possible to be engaged in SR&ED activities if you have to reinvent the wheel, so to speak, for your business. Where a certain product or process is available only to a limited number of companies and you have to reinvent that product or process on your own, you may still qualify for SR&ED tax credits. However, if the technology is common knowledge, then your expenditures would not normally qualify.

SR&ED does not include research and development in any of the humanities or in product style changes. For example, market research, sales promotion, quality control, routine data collection, and ongoing style changes would not qualify for SR&ED. Nor would research and development for a new book or course qualify for the tax credit. The activity must be science-oriented and result in a technological improvement or advancement.

There is a fine line between routine enhancements of a product that would not qualify for SR&ED tax credits and a technological advancement that would qualify. Consider, for example, an ice cream maker that adds a new flavour to its list of ice cream flavours. Yes, research and development had to go into the creation of that new flavour. But the basic process is already established. It is just a matter of trying different ingredients until they get a tasty product.

On the other hand, consider the ice cream maker that, for the first time ever, developed frozen yogurt. Here is a product that may taste similar to ice cream but is significantly different. This is an advancement in technology for the ice cream business. The research and development that went into developing frozen yogurt for the first time should qualify for research and development. However, if the making of frozen yogurt is now common knowledge for those in the industry, a company developing their own brand of frozen yogurt would not qualify for SR&ED unless they are improving the technology somehow.

In many cases, it is difficult to determine if a certain activity will qualify for SR&ED. Fortunately Canada Revenue Agency have listened to the concerns of businesses and have developed the Preclaim Project Review Service or PCPR. The service is meant to give the taxpayer an assessment up front as to whether or not their project will likely qualify for SR&ED tax credits. The program is entirely optional. By using it however, you can save time and money by knowing up front if your project qualifies for the SR&ED tax credits. In addition, CRA has developed the First Time Claimant Service, which provides information about the SR&ED program. For more information you can visit the SR&ED web site at www.ccra. gc.ca/sred. Overall, CRA is attempting to make the program easier for you to obtain information and to apply it in your business.

TAX BEATER

Consider using the Preclaim Project Review Service to save time and money in determining if your project qualifies.

What Are the Tax Benefits of Claiming SR&ED?

If you are engaged in SR&ED activities, you can enjoy several tax advantages and benefits. The tax benefits are a result of receiving very favourable tax treatments regarding deducting SR&ED expenditures as well as being eligible for investment tax credits on these expenditures.

Delay Deducting Expenses

All expenditures that relate to SR&ED activities are eligible to be included in a pool of expenditures. This includes both expense and capital expenditures. You can deduct this pool of expenditures basically whenever you want. For example, if you are incurring losses and you can't make use of additional losses, you can delay deducting the pool of expenditures. Usually, expense items must be deducted and added to your loss carry forward if your business is losing money. However, SR&ED expense items can be added to the pool and deducted when it suits your tax planning. This is especially important when you consider that business loss carry forwards have a limited ten year life, if incurred in a taxation year ending after March 22, 2004, 20 years if incurred in 2006 or a later taxation year, or seven years if they arose in a taxation year before March 22, 2004, and then they expire.

> **TAX BEATER**
> Delay deducting SR&ED expenses to reduce risk of loss carry forwards expiring.

Speed Up Deducting Capital Expenditures

With capital items, you are normally restricted to a slow depreciation of the expenditure over time. However, if the capital expenditure relates to SR&ED, you are eligible to expense the item all in one year. This again provides significant flexibility in planning your tax strategy and minimizing your taxes.

> **TAX BEATER**
> Deduct SR&ED capital expenditures all in one year.

Claim 20% Investment Tax Credits

As mentioned earlier, SR&ED expenditures also qualify for investment tax credits. As an individual or member of a partnership, all SR&ED expenditures, whether capital or expense items, qualify for a 20% investment tax credit rate. (This rate use to be 30%, for individuals and members of a partnership that lived in the four Atlantic provinces or in the Gaspé Peninsula and if the expenditure was made before 1995.)

Claim 35% Investment Tax Credits

For taxation years ending before February 26, 2008, if the SR&ED activities are engaged within a small Canadian corporation, the tax credit increases to 35% on the first $2,000,000 of expenditures and 20% thereafter. As part of the 2008 federal budget, the government proposed to increase the $2,000,000 limit to $3,000,000. As such, for taxation years ending after February 26, 2008 if a small Canadian corporation is engaged in SR&ED activities, it is entitled to a 35% tax credit on the first $3,000,000 of expenditures and 20% thereafter. If your business is heavily engaged in SR&ED activities, it may be worth considering incorporating your business, given the extra 15% investment tax credit available to small companies. However, the extra tax credit should be weighed against all the other pros and cons of incorporating as discussed in Round 5.

Claim 40% Refund of Investment Tax Credits

Another advantage of the SR&ED program is that the investment tax credits can be refunded, even if there is no tax liability. For individuals and partnerships, 40% of the investment tax credit not used to reduce the current year's income tax liability can be refunded on your personal tax return. The balance can then be carried back or forward to reduce past and future tax liabilities. The 40% refund provides a cash incentive even in a year where you would not normally be paying any tax.

Claim 100% Refund of Investment Tax Credits

For small corporations, the 40% refund of investment tax credits increases to 100%. In other words, despite the fact that a corporation may have no taxable income, you can still receive a refund of up to 100% of the investment tax credits calculated in the year. This provides another incentive to incorporate a business that is engaging in SR&ED.

> **TAX BEATER**
>
> Consider incorporating your business to receive a 100% refund of investment tax credits.

How Do You Claim a SR&ED Tax Benefit?

In order to qualify for the favourable tax treatments under the SR&ED program, you must complete and submit to Canada Revenue Agency form T661, "Claim for Scientific Research and Experimental Development Expenditures Carried on in Canada," in addition to the form T2038 discussed previously. If this is your first submission of a SR&ED project, Canada Revenue Agency will request that an expert in your industry review your project confidentially to ensure that it meets the government guidelines for qualification. If the scientific expert approves the project, a tax auditor will review the mathematical calculations of the claim. Once this is complete, the government will process the refunds.

If you have made previous submissions for SR&ED projects that have received approvals, then the process is normally streamlined or fast-tracked. Your first claim will be reviewed carefully, 100% of the time. My experience has been, however, that the auditors are very helpful and do not audit other aspects of your business while they're there. It may be one of the few times that you don't have to worry when the taxman calls to see your records.

How Long Do I Have to File the SR&ED Forms?

To be eligible to claim SR&ED tax deductions and tax credits, you must file the form T661 on time. If you are late in filing the form T661, you will lose forever the ability to claim the tax benefits of the SR&ED expenditures for that period.

TAX BEATER

File your SR&ED forms before the deadline or lose the tax benefits forever.

Determining when the T661 form is required to be filed is not an easy task. It use to be that you had up to ten years to file the form. Then in the February 22, 1994 budget, the government decided to dramatically reduce the time frame. This left everyone scrambling to submit claims for old SR&ED activities by September 13, 1994.

For taxation years commencing after 1995, the filing deadline for the T661 is twelve months after your filing due date for the year you incurred the SR&ED expenditures. Therefore, if your sole proprietorship had a January 2008 year-end, you would have until June 15, 2010, to file the T661. Your January 2008 year-end is included in your 2008 personal tax return which is due by June 15, 2009. You have up until twelve months from June 15, 2009, to file the T661.

For corporations, the filing due date of the corporate tax returns is six months after the year-end of the company. Therefore, if a company had a January 2008 year-end, the filing deadline for their SR&ED claim would be July 31, 2009. The corporate tax returns are due six months after January 31, 2008, being July 31, 2008, and the SR&ED claim is due twelve months after the filing deadline or July 31, 2009.

In the February 18, 1997 budget, the government expanded this deadline to include all investment tax credit claims, whether they be SR&ED claims or Atlantic Canada ITC's.

What Happens When I Receive the Refund?

Investment tax credits must be applied to reduce your pool of SR&ED expenditures in the year after you apply for the credits. As discussed earlier, all SR&ED expenditures are placed in a pool and deducted at your discretion. If after deducting the refunded investment tax credits there is a negative balance in the pool, you will need to add the negative balance to your income.

For example, if you had SR&ED expenditures of $10,000 and you deducted $8,500 in your business, the balance of $1,500 you can carry forward in your pool. On the $10,000 of SR&ED expenditures you would have claimed an investment tax credit of $2,000. The full $2,000 investment tax credit must be applied to reduce your pool, which will leave a negative balance in the pool of $500. This negative balance of $500 must be included in your income.

This procedure is consistent with the idea that investment tax credits must be included in income or reduce a CCA class to which the tax credit relates in the year after the year you reduce your tax liability for the tax credit. However, with SR&ED investment tax credits, they reduce the SR&ED expenditure pool, which can then delay the timing of including the credits in income.

The inclusion of the investment tax credits in income is often forgotten by many taxpayers. This is especially important if you are hiring someone to review your files to submit a claim for SR&ED tax credits. Very often the fee structure for this work is based on a percentage of the investment tax refund. However, rarely is any consideration given to the tax implications of the refund. If 40% of an investment tax credit refund is paid to the firm making the claim and 50% is paid to the government in additional taxes, not much is left over for yourself.

One final comment about SR&ED expenditures. This is a very complex area in tax. There are many possible ways of legitimately increasing the amount of your investment tax credits. In this Round I have tried to cover some of the more important tax aspects that you should be aware of. If you have the possibility of significant SR&ED expenditures, you should seek the assistance of a professional tax coach. The tax credits are lucrative and worth the time spent.

What Is the Apprenticeship Job Creation Tax Credit?

Various provinces already offer some type of apprenticeship tax credit. Apprenticeship tax credits are tax credits available to businesses that hire and train apprentices in various trades. In 2006, the federal government implemented a new

TAX BEATER

Remember that investment tax credits are included in income when hiring someone to submit your claim.

TAX BEATER

Determine whether you are eligible to claim an Apprenticeship Job Creation Tax Credit for any new employees.

Apprenticeship Job Creation Tax Credit. This tax credit is aimed at encouraging employers to hire new apprentices in eligible trades.

Generally, an employer will be able to claim a federal non-refundable tax credit equal to 10% of the eligible salaries and wages payable to eligible apprentices in respect of employment after May 1, 2006. The maximum credit is $2,000 per year for each eligible apprentice. The government considers eligible salaries and wages to be those payable by the employer to an eligible apprentice for the apprentices' employment in Canada in the tax year and during the first 24 months of the apprenticeship. It does not include remuneration based on profits, bonuses, and taxable benefits. An eligible apprentice is an individual who is working in a prescribed trade in the first two years of their apprenticeship contract. This contract must be registered with a federal, provincial or territorial government under an apprenticeship program designed to certify or license individuals in a particular trade. The government has indicated that a prescribed trade includes trades currently listed as "Red Seal Trades." At the time of publication, a total of 49 trades were considered "Red Seal Trades." A listing of the most up-to-date "Red Seal Trades" can be obtained on-line at http://www.red-seal.ca. In order to claim this tax credit on your tax return, you will have to complete either Form T2038(IND), *"Investment Tax Credit (Individuals)"* or Form T2SCH31, *"Investment Tax Credit—Corporations."*

If a business cannot benefit from this tax credit in any particular year, and thereby has unused tax credits, they may carry-back the unused credits three years and forward twenty to reduce federal taxes owing in those years.

What is the Investment Tax Credit for Child Care Spaces

On December 14, 2007, new legislation came into effect related to the creation of child care spaces. As part of the 2007 federal budget, the government put forth a proposal for a new credit for the creation of child care spaces. Essentially, employers that create child care spaces in a licensed child care facility for the benefit of their employee's children or a combination of their employee's children and other children, will qualify for a non-refundable investment tax credit equal to 25% of eligible child care space expenditures incurred after March 18, 2007, to a maximum investment tax credit of $10,000 per child care space created. The amount of the credit can be used to reduce federal taxes payable for the taxation year. As is the case, with other investment tax credits, any unused credits can be carried back 3 years and forward 20 years.

However, it is important to note that this investment tax credit is available to a taxpayer only if the provision of the child care space is ancillary to one or more businesses of the taxpayer carried on in Canada that do not otherwise include the provision of child care spaces. In other words, the credit does not apply to child care businesses such as those carried on by child day care centres.

Surviving a Visit from the Taxman

The objective of the previous rounds has been to show you ways to reduce your tax bill using the existing set of rules that we all have to follow. By knowing a little bit about these rules and knowing how to use them to your advantage, you can save significant tax dollars. But what if the tax department doesn't agree with you. What if their interpretation of the rules is different from yours, or say that a particular rule doesn't apply in your case. What can they do? And more importantly, what can you do?

This round will look at the different steps of a Canada Revenue Agency audit and what rights you have under the tax system. Knowing the rules of this game can mean the difference between victory and utter defeat.

What Happens After I File My Tax Return?

The Assessment Process

After you file your tax return, Canada Revenue Agency's computers will conduct a number of tests on your return and will issue you what is called an *Assessment Notice*. The assessment notice is typically two or three pages in length, will include information such as how much income you earned, how much tax you paid, how much you can contribute to your RRSP next year, and what balance you still owe to the government, if any, for the current year's taxes. Also included with the assessment is a cheque if you were expecting a refund and you did not request direct deposit.

At the assessment notice stage, typically, the only checks that the tax department has done is to ensure that your tax return is mathematically correct and confirmed some of your deductions to available carryforward information, like how much you were eligible to deduct for RRSP purposes. Barring unusual circumstances, you are issued the assessment notice and either a refund cheque (or direct deposit), a request for additional funds, or an indication that your account is paid in full with no balance owing.

This assessment notice is a very important piece of correspondence. It tells you if the government has agreed with the way you filed your tax return or not. It is on the assessment notice that the tax department will indicate the amount of any interest and penalties that were assessed. If the balance owing or due as a refund on the assessment notice differs from what you expected, you should enquire further. The government's computers have been known to make errors at this stage. It may be a misunderstanding that can be easily cleared up. So review your assessment notice carefully for any unexpected surprises. It could make a big difference to the amount of tax you have to pay.

TAX BEATER
Review your assessment notice to ensure you're not paying more tax than necessary.

The Audit Process

Just because you have received an assessment notice from Canada Revenue Agency agreeing with how you filed your tax return, does not necessarily mean you're out of the woods. The government has up to three years from the time of issuing you the assessment notice to go back and audit that year.

Longer if you provide them with a waiver for the particular year.

According to Canada Revenue Agency's mission statement, their objective is to promote compliance with Canada's tax, trade, and border legislation and regulations. Their main tool is the audit process. The majority of taxpayers file relatively simple tax returns with mostly T4 and T5 income. These tax returns do not represent a large compliance risk since tax is withheld at source on the T4 income and the amounts are easily verifiable. Accordingly, many taxpayers who report this type of income may never be audited by the tax department or have any dealings with a tax auditor.

Taxpayers who operate small businesses represent a greater risk of non-compliance to the government. Accordingly, more effort is placed on auditing taxpayers that report business or professional income. This is not to say that if you operate a small business you will be audited. There are hundreds of thousands of small businesses across Canada and Canada Revenue Agency can't audit them all. But your chances of being audited are increased when you report self-employed income.

If you are selected for audit, depending on the circumstances, the tax department may perform what is called a desk audit or perform a field audit. With a desk audit, a tax auditor may request that you provide supporting documentation for specific questions he or she has concerning your tax return. For example, they may request support for moving expenses or medical expenses claimed.

A field audit typically involves a tax auditor official actually visiting your premises and reviewing your records on site. They will normally contact you to set up a mutually convenient time and will typically review more than one year at a time. Alternatively, if your business is relatively small, they may request that you bring your records to them and they will conduct their audit at their office instead of your office.

To minimize your disruption you should enquire up front what records they wish to review and what information they

TAX BEATER

Recommend having Canada Revenue Agency conduct their audit at your accountant's office to minimize disruption and possibly tax.

will require. Having this information ready for when they arrive can speed up their audit and save you time and money. Additionally, if you have an accountant, you might suggest that the tax official perform their audit at your accountants office, if everyone is agreeable. This will minimize your disruption. As well it may help to have a trained, objective party answer the tax auditor's questions on your behalf.

The Reassessment

If, after completing their field audit, Canada Revenue Agency disagrees with your calculation of income, they will typically issue you a letter detailing the proposed adjustments to your tax return. They will also normally give you 30 days to respond to this letter, unless further time is requested. It is at this point that you should argue your case with the tax auditor. Nothing is final yet and if the issue is a matter of interpretation, you may be able to sway the auditors opinion or negotiate a better result. This is not the time to ignore the letter. This is your last chance to argue your case cheaply. From here on in, if you want to fight the tax department's decision, it will cost you a lot more money and time. So review the letter, discuss it with your tax coach and meet with the tax auditor to go over any areas with which you disagree.

TAX BEATER

Save time and money by reviewing in detail Canada Revenue Agency's proposed adjustments.

Once the issues contained in the proposed adjustments letter are either agreed with or you and the auditor agree to disagree, a *Notice of Reassessment* is issued. The notice of reassessment will indicate the changes to the income and deduction numbers as appropriate and it will show the new tax calculation, any interest and penalties owing and the total tax owing to the government or to be refunded. If more than one taxation year is being reassessed, then typically the balance owing or refunded will be carried forward from year to year so that the most recent notice of reassessment's balance owing or refund will represent accumulated balances of all the years being reassessed.

What If I Disagree with the Notice of Reassessment?

There are occasions when Canada Revenue Agency will not issue you a letter of proposed adjustments. For example, this will be the case if they review your tax return and find that you forgot to include a T5 or T4 slip. In these cases, they will just issue you a notice of reassessment, without warning.

If you disagree with a notice of reassessment issued to you that was either received after an audit where you have already met with the tax department or issued to you unannounced, you have two possible responses. If it is an obvious error by the tax department the best thing to do is call them and explain why you feel the notice of reassessment is incorrect. It may be a simple mistake which a quick phone call can easily solve.

If, on the other hand, the issue is not an obvious error but more a matter of a difference in interpretation, then a quick phone call is not likely to help. Instead, your next option is to file a *Notice of Objection*. The notice of objection is simply a letter that you write to the Chief of Appeals of your local district taxation office. In the letter you provide details as to why you disagree with the notice of assessment or reassessment as applicable. At one time you were required to complete form T400A when you wanted to file a notice of objection. This is no longer required, however, it may be advisable. By completing form T400A you will ensure that you have all of the pertinent information and Canada Revenue Agency will know for sure that you wish to begin the formal appeals process.

TAX BEATER

Complete Form T400A for notice of objections to ensure Canada Revenue Agency processes your objection properly.

You have only a limited time frame for which you are eligible to file a notice of objection. If you delay and miss this time frame, you will not be eligible to appeal your case. For an individual, you have the later of 90 days from the filing of the notice of (re)assessment or one year from the due date of the tax return. For example, if your 2007 tax return was due for filing on June 15, 2008, and you received a notice of assessment that you disagreed with in August 2008, you will

TAX BEATER

File your notice of objection on time to keep your appeal rights alive.

have until June 15, 2009 (one year from the due date of your 2007 tax return), to file your notice of objection. On the other hand, if you received a notice of reassessment for your 2006 tax return dated November 30, 2008, you will have until February 28, 2009, to file your notice of objection. For a corporation, you have to file a notice of objection within 90 days of the date of the assessment or reassessment notice.

Once the notice of objection is received by Canada Revenue Agency it is given to the appeals branch of the district taxation office. The appeals branch will provide an independent review of your situation. They may request additional information or an interview. After they have reviewed your case they will either issue a new reassessment notice or confirm the original assessment or reassessment.

If you still don't agree at this point, your next course of action is to appeal to the *Tax Court of Canada*. Here you have a choice: you can either appeal using the general procedure or the informal procedure. The general procedure requires you to hire a lawyer to represent you. If the tax amount in dispute is greater than $12,000 federally, then you will have to use the general procedure.

With the informal procedure, you can represent yourself or have a friend, your tax coach, or a lawyer represent you. This can be a less costly procedure and less formal. However, it is still a complicated procedure. You would be wise to have some assistance from someone who knows the system and can assist you competently.

If you win or loose at this level, you or Canada Revenue Agency may be able to appeal to the Federal Court of Appeal. If you or Canada Revenue Agency are unsuccessful at this level, in very rare circumstances you can appeal to the Supreme Court of Canada. Very few tax cases make it all the way to the Supreme Court of Canada.

The appeal process can be very costly and can take years to complete. Save yourself time and money by addressing the issues early on and seek the advice of your tax coach. Make sure you pick your fights wisely. A wrong move here can cost you a lot of money and aggravation.

Should I Pay Tax That Is Under Dispute?

Canada Revenue Agency has assessed you tax which you are appealing. Should you pay the tax liability or wait until a decision has been reached on your appeal? Generally, upon filing a notice of objection, the tax department will stop collection proceedings. However, it may still be advisable to pay the outstanding tax. In most cases the decision boils down to how confident are you that you will win and can you afford to pay the tax.

If you don't pay the tax and you lose your appeal, you will not only owe the tax liability but also interest that has been compounding daily. And as discussed earlier, this interest is not tax deductible. On the other hand, if you pay the outstanding tax, you stop the interest clock. And if you win, the government will pay you interest on the amount you overpaid. Of course, you will have to include the interest as income on your tax return in the year that you receive it.

TAX BEATER

Stop the interest clock by paying disputed tax liabilities.

If you can afford to pay the tax, generally the wise thing to do is pay it even if you don't agree with the calculation. Paying the tax does not represent an admission that the tax department is correct. It in no way affects your right to appeal. It does however stop the interest clock which over time can add up to a lot of money.

What If I Have Discovered an Error in a Prior Year's Tax Return?

If you review your tax returns and find that you made an error in a previous years return, you will generally be allowed to request Canada Revenue Agency to go back and make the change. Even though technically the tax department does not have to adjust a prior year tax return without you filing a notice of objection, administratively, Canada Revenue Agency will normally make the requested adjustment. You must however, make your request within three years from the date on the original notice of assessment.

To make a change to a prior year tax return, the tax department would prefer that you file Form T1-ADJ, T1 Adjustment Request. You file a separate form for each tax year in question. Canada Revenue Agency prefers the use of the T1-ADJ form over filing amended tax returns.

Canada Revenue Agency will generally not allow you to go back and make a change to a prior years tax return if you are changing an optional deduction and the change affects the income for that year. A typical example might be to increase or decrease the amount of capital cost allowance (CCA) claimed in a prior year. You can, however, change your CCA claim for a prior year if it has no effect on income. This might be the case where you decrease the CCA claim in one class and increase it in another class so there is no effect on income. Additionally, if you file a notice of objection within the allowed time frame as discussed above, the tax department will normally allow you to make the CCA adjustment. As well, if a prior year tax return is changed due to the correction of other errors, then the tax department will normally allow you to change permissible deductions for that year.

As mentioned above, the law stipulates that you can only go back three years to make an adjustment to a prior years tax return. After the three-year period, the tax returns are considered *statute-barred*. However, in 1991 the government introduced rules that enabled Canada Revenue Agency to reassess personal tax returns back to 1985 if requested by the taxpayer. Under the old rules, if after three years you realized you missed a deduction or hadn't yet filed a tax return, the tax department was not required to issue a refund. Even though you were entitled to the amount and the tax department agreed. If you had not made the request before the three years were up then you didn't get the refund. A severe penalty for procrastination. Corporate tax returns are, however, still subject to the three year restriction.

TAX BEATER

Request a refund of missed deductions.

The rules surrounding the time frame for requesting adjustments changed again in 2004. These new rules have limited the time frame for processing adjustments to a ten-year period. The new ten-year time frame is in effect for all requests made after 2004. Therefore, if at some point during 2007 you discovered that there was an error on a previous years tax return, you could only request adjustments for tax returns dating back to 1997. In most cases, Canada Revenue Agency will go back, make the changes you request, and issue you a refund. This assumes of course that you can substantiate the changes and the tax department agrees to them. As well, if you have not filed a tax return in the past and you are expecting a refund, Canada Revenue Agency will refund you any amounts owing. This is a significant win for the taxpayer.

TAX BEATER

Review old tax years for potential tax adjustments before it is too late.

Is There Any Relief If I Have Never Filed a Tax Return or Did Not Report All of My Income?

Canada Revenue Agency's stated objective is to promote compliance with the *Income Tax Act*. The government wants to encourage all taxpayers to file their tax returns on time. If you have never filed a tax return or you did not report all of your income on tax returns you did file and you have not been approached by Canada Revenue Agency, then consider contacting the tax department and state that you wish to make a *Voluntary Disclosure*.

TAX BEATER

Make a voluntary disclosure and avoid penalty charges.

To encourage taxpayers to come forward, Canada Revenue Agency will often waive the penalties associated with late filing your tax return, not including all of your income in your tax returns or claiming ineligible expenses if you make a voluntary disclosure. You will still be charged interest and will have to pay any tax owing, but you may be able to avoid significant penalty charges. To qualify you must meet a number of criteria:

1. You must initiate the contact with Canada Revenue Agency. If the tax department contacts you first, the deal's off and you will likely be charged penalties.

2. There must be sufficient and complete information for the years under question. You will need to provide to the tax department sufficient information to substantiate your income and expense numbers. You won't need to provide this information immediately. In fact, you should first contact Canada Revenue Agency and then work out a mutually acceptable time frame to provide them with the details.

3. The CRA must be in a position to apply some type of penalty. As an example, the penalty may be a late filing or failure to file penalty. If a penalty does not apply, you cannot seek relief under the Voluntary Disclosures Program, you can however still disclose the information to the CRA and it will be handled through the normal processing procedures.

4. The information being disclosed must be at least one year past due or less than one year past due where the disclosure is to correct a previously filed return. For example, assume you had not filed tax returns for the years 2001 to 2005, and on November 10, 2006 you filed all of these returns under the Voluntary Disclosures Program. Although the 2005 tax return is less than one year past due (it would have been due on April 30, 2006), the CRA will consider the 2005 return as part of the disclosure, assuming that all of the required conditions have been met. However, the 2005 tax return would not be considered under the Voluntary Disclosures Program if it were the only return being filed. In this circumstance, the 2005 tax return would be handled through the Canada Revenue Agency's normal processing procedures.

If you decide to make use of the Voluntary Disclosure Program, you must make a written submission outlining the relevant details using Form RC199, "Taxpayer Agreement" to initiate the process. If your submission is accepted, then you must pay the outstanding tax and interest amount or work out acceptable payment terms. Be aware that the tax department could go back and assess penalties if you renege on your part of the deal and don't pay your tax bill after you come forward.

When you approach the tax department, negotiate with them the number of years they would like you to go back. Depending on how long you have not filed a tax return, they may agree to waive some old years just to bring you back into the system. This is not always negotiable. However, depending on your circumstances, it can represent a significant savings if you don't have to file for some of the outstanding years.

The voluntary disclosure rules can also apply for GST returns that have never been filed or that have been filed with incomplete information. Once again however, you must approach the tax department before they approach you.

> **TAX BEATER**
>
> Save tax and hassles by negotiating the number of years for filing tax returns.

Can Penalty and Interest Charges Be Reduced?

If you have been charged a penalty or interest, consider requesting to have the penalty and interest charges reversed. Canada Revenue Agency will, on occasion, reverse these charges. However, you must provide them with an exceptional reason why you were unable to comply with the law, resulting in the assessing of penalties and interest. Canada Revenue Agency has cited the following examples of circumstances which may be acceptable in reversing penalties and interest, if these circumstances prevented a taxpayer from complying with the law:

1. natural or human-made disasters such as a flood or a fire

2. civil disturbances or disruptions in services such as a postal strike

3. a serious illness or accident

4. serious emotional or mental distress such as a death in the immediate family.

As well, penalties and interest may be waived if Canada Revenue Agency delayed in informing you of an amount owing, or if you were relying on material made available to the public and the material contained incorrect information.

TAX BEATER

Consider requesting Canada Revenue Agency to reverse interest and penalties.

If you receive incorrect advice from Canada Revenue Agency, you shouldn't be charged interest or penalties. If the tax department tells you that you don't have to make instalments and then later charges you late instalment interest, you should be able to get that interest reversed.

In addition, if Canada Revenue Agency makes an error in processing, interest and penalties should not be charged on the error. Or if the tax department delays in providing the necessary information to make the appropriate instalment or payments, you may be able to get the interest and penalty reversed.

One other situation where it may be possible to waive interest and penalties is in severe hardship cases. If you are having severe difficulty in paying your outstanding taxes, the government may waive the interest and penalties in order to recover the outstanding tax liability.

In summary, don't just give up if you have been assessed interest and penalties. In the right circumstances, you may be able to get them reversed.

What Are Some Do's and Don't's If I Get Audited?

So you've been selected for audit. If you have reported all of your income and have been reasonable with your business expenses, you should have nothing to worry about. They may have selected you at random, because of something unusual that is going on in your tax return or because of your industry. Whatever the reason, in many cases there is nothing to fear. If you do get selected for audit here are some things you should and some things you should not do:

- Do respond promptly to Canada Revenue Agency phone calls and/or correspondence. Ignoring them will not make them go away. It will only make them more intolerant later when you try to negotiate with them.

- Do cooperate by providing them with the information they request. Ask them why they are requesting the information. The tax department does have the right to review your records to substantiate information you have reported on your tax return. However, they do not have a right to engage in a "fishing exhibition."

- Do offer to have the tax auditor review your records at your accountant's office. This will reduce your disruption and may make the audit go smoother.

- Do review in detail their proposed adjustments. Tax auditors do make mistakes.

- Do attempt to negotiate on grey or interpretative matters. Where the rules are not black and white, the auditor may be willing to give a little, depending on the circumstances.

- Do seek professional tax help. Not all audits go smoothly and mistakes can be made. Misinterpretion of the facts is quite common. A tax professional can help you make sure the auditor understands your business and your transactions in the best possible light.

- Don't provide more information than requested unless it helps your case. As mentioned earlier, ask what the auditor needs and cooperate. But if they don't ask for some information, don't volunteer it unless it helps your case. There is no sense in making a career out of the audit of your business.

- Don't accept the word of the auditor as gospel. The auditor's interpretation of certain legislation may be right, but then again it may be wrong. Check with your tax coach or ask to speak with the auditor's supervisor if you feel that there may be an error.

- Don't delay in filing a notice of objection. You don't necessarily want to file a notice of objection if you have an open dialogue with the tax auditor on some contentious points. However, keep in mind your deadlines and make sure you file your objection before you run out of time.

The audit experience is rarely a pleasant one. However, it doesn't have to be painful. If you follow the rules and are not too aggressive, you can win this round with a little bit of luck.

And the Winner Is...

Just like winning a prize fight, to "Beat the Taxman" takes know-how, determination, discipline, and a little bit of luck. The previous Rounds contain an arsenal of moves that can be used to reduce your tax liability. Some moves are simple, like paying your taxes and instalments on time. Other ideas are slightly more complex, like using corporations to defer tax or applying for scientific research and experimental development tax credits. However, they all have one thing in common: Used properly they can save you tax dollars.

Once you have the know-how, the next step is to take this information and act on it. In some cases this may require more knowledge. You may need to seek the advice of a tax coach. Or it may just require some clarification with the tax department on the application of the rules to your particular business. Either way, if in doubt seek additional knowledge and expert advice.

Once you are sure that the idea applies to you and your business, it will take determination on your part to ensure that the tax savings will occur. This may mean a change in the way you do things. Maybe this will mean recording the business transactions more frequently. Maybe you will have to procrastinate less and get documents filed on time. Maybe you will need to sit down with your banker and discuss ways to finance your business to ensure you are maximizing your tax deductions. Whatever the changes may be, you will need to be determined in your approach.

But determination alone is not enough. Just because you are determined to win the fight, doesn't necessarily mean you will. You also need to be disciplined. I am not talking about an onerous kind of discipline that will require all of your focus and concentration. Instead, I simply refer to a tax-savings discipline: A conscious intention to conduct your business in a manner that will maximize your tax savings and business profits. When these two ideals clash, you must choose which is more important. But the key is remembering that significant tax saving occurs through a disciplined approach throughout the year. You don't train for a fight in one day. Similarly you don't save taxes one day of the year.

And finally, I wish you the best of luck in your business endeavours and your tax savings fight.

Quick Reference to Tax Beaters

1. Deduct the cost of this book and save. (pg. xvi)

2. Prepare and periodically revise your business plan to support any business losses. (pg. 6)

3. Report all legitimate business expenses even if you incur persistent losses. (pg. 7)

4. Record all business-related expenses between startup and your first sale. (pg. 7)

5. Don't spend money on your business before official startup. (pg. 8)

6. The general rule: All reasonable business-related expenses are tax deductible. (pg. 8)

7. Know and follow the rules for self-employment. (pg. 9)

8. Record all expenses to save tax dollars. (pg. 11)

9. Accurate records can help you prove your case to Canada Revenue Agency. (pg. 12)

10. Make sure that you have an up-to-date back up of any electronic records. (pg. 14)

11. Even without a receipt you can still claim an expense. (pg. 14)

12. Where no description shows on a receipt, itemize the purchase yourself. (pg. 15)

13. Record your transactions weekly so you don't forget a business expense. (pg. 16)

14. Use a double-entry record-keeping system to avoid costly mistakes. (pg. 16)

15. By timing purchases and sales at year-end, the cash method can save you tax. (pg. 22)

16. Speed up tax savings by choosing a December year-end when your business is losing money during the early years. (pg. 28)

17. Defer tax by staying with a non-December year-end if your income is increasing. (pg. 28)

18. Save tax by changing to a December year-end if income from an established business is decreasing. (pg. 29)

19. Elect to include income in your first year of business to reduce income taxed at high tax rates. (pg. 33)

20. Elect to defer income that will be taxed in the current year at the highest tax rate. (pg. 34)

21. Maximize income in lower tax levels and minimize income in higher tax levels. (pg. 38)

22. Save significant tax dollars by legally allocating income among family members. (pg. 41)

23. Lend money to your spouse or minor child at a prescribed interest rate and save tax dollars. (pg. 41)

24. Invest money lent to children in capital gain producing assets and avoid attribution. (pg. 42)

25. Invest child tax benefit receipts in the name of your child and save tax dollars. (pg. 42)

26. Lending money to a family member to finance a small or home-based business is allowable income splitting. (pg. 43)

27. Save as much as $3,700 per child, per year, by putting your children on salary. (pg. 43)

28. File tax returns for your children and build RRSP contribution room. (pg. 45)

29. Pay a dependent parent a salary. (pg. 45)

30. If your income is in excess of $36,378 and your spouse is in a lower bracket, pay your spouse a salary. (pg. 46)

31. Salary for family members must be reasonable and for services rendered. (pg. 47)

32. Apply to have your family member EI exempt. (pg. 49)

33. Apply for refunds of EI paid to family members for up to three prior years. (pg. 50)

34. If you do not already have employees, consider making your family member(s) partners. This avoids costs and headaches involved in having a payroll. (pg. 51)

35. Make spousal RRSP contributions to save taxes today and tomorrow. (pg. 52)

36. Hold off deducting your RRSP contribution in a year where your income is low and you expect next year's income to be high. (pg. 53)

37. Claim business losses on your tax return to receive an immediate tax refund or reduce future tax liabilities. (pg. 54)

38. File your loss carry-back election on time in order to get your refund. (pg. 54)

39. Apply a loss to the third prior taxation year before it is too late. (pg. 55)

40. Apply a loss over the past three years to minimize higher income levels. (pg. 55)

41. Carry losses forward if next year's income is expected to be high. (pg. 55)

42. Claim a reserve for income that has been received but in return for which services have not been rendered or goods have not been shipped. (pg. 56)

43. Claim reserves on questionable receivables. (pg. 56)

44. Defer claiming CCA on fast write-off assets in low income years to get more dollar for your deduction. (pg. 57)

45. Use a corporation to smooth income from year-to-year and save tax. (pg. 58)

46. Declare bonuses at year-end to defer tax. (pg. 58)

47. Highly successful small-business entrepreneurs should consider using a corporation to defer up to $116,000 a year in taxes. (pg. 59)

48. Save time and money by choosing the proper business structure. (pg. 62)

49. To save money and avoid hassles, develop a partnership agreement. (pg. 65)

50. Save taxes in start-up years where you have losses by using the sole proprietorship or partnership structure. (pg. 67)

51. Defer up to 28% in taxes by using a corporation properly. (pg. 68)

52. Distribute corporate retained profits to shareholders when personal income is low. (pg. 69)

53. Save thousands of dollars by selling shares that qualify for the $500,000 capital gains exemption. (pg. 71)

54. Crystallize your capital gains exemption on QSBC shares to ensure its tax benefits for the future. (pg. 72)

55. Include your family as shareholders and increase the tax savings on a sale. (pg. 73)

56. Save taxes by transferring profitable businesses into a corporation and keeping losing businesses as sole proprietorships. (pg. 78)

57. Register for GST if you are selling zero-rated goods and services to obtain refund of GST on purchases. (pg. 81)

58. Register for the GST and increase profits. (pg. 82)

59. Register for the GST at start up and claim input tax credits on all your business purchases. (pg. 83)

60. Reduce tax and simplify GST record-keeping by using the "Quick Method." (pg. 85)

61. Maximize your GST savings by claiming the 1% reduction. (pg. 86)

62. Remember to claim input tax credits on capital purchases when using the "Quick Method." (pg. 86)

63. Claim forgotten input tax credits before the four-year limitation is up. (pg. 86)

64. Request GST information be included on purchase invoices to save money and hassles. (pg. 88)

65. Remember to include input tax credits on capital purchases used in your business. (pg. 90)

66. Claim ITCs on assets purchased prior to registering for the GST and still being used in the business. (pg. 90)

67. Claim ITCs on services that were paid prior to registering but were used after registering. (pg. 91)

68. Claim Input Tax Credits on personal capital property used more than 50% of the time in your taxable business. (pg. 91)

69. Claim Input Tax Credits on general operating expenses for items used more than 10% of the time in a taxable business. (pg. 94)

70. Speed up Input Tax Credit refunds by electing to file quarterly or monthly. (pg. 96)

71. Reduce hassles and reporting costs by filing GST returns only as required. (pg. 97)

72. Remit your GST on time and reduce the amount you pay. (pg. 98)

73. Make sure all of the returns your business is required to file have in fact been filed in order to have your refunds processed quickly. (pg. 100)

74. Remember to request a refund of the GST and PST on accounts receivable that you have written off. (pg. 100)

75. Remember to charge GST on the sale of used capital assets. (pg. 102)

76. Remember to claim ITCs on gifts or free samples you provide to your customers. (pg. 102)

77. Be careful to charge the HST on sales to participating provinces or else you may be paying the tax. (pg. 103)

78. File your tax return and pay any balance owing by April 30 to avoid being charged interest. (pg. 108)

79. Reduce the money you pay the government by paying and filing your tax return on time. (pg. 109)

80. Pay your tax instalments as required to reduce your overall costs and increase profits. (pg. 112)

81. Follow the "No-Calculation Option" when your income is stable or rising to minimize the amount of pre-paid tax. (pg. 114)

82. Increase cash flow by electing to use alternative instalment options. (pg. 115)

83. Use the "Current-Year Instalment Option" in years of declining income to maximize cash flow and personal wealth. (pg. 116)

84. If you miss an instalment payment, catch up your instalments and prepay the next instalment to reduce or eliminate the non-deductible instalment interest charge. (pg. 117)

85. Properly withhold and remit payroll taxes on time. (pg. 119)

86. Increase cash flow and save time by electing to reduce your payroll remittance frequency. (pg. 120)

87. File employee information returns by the end of February to avoid significant penalties. (pg. 120)

88. Make a reasonable effort to obtain employee SINs or be charged a penalty. (pg. 121)

89. If required, submit contract payment information to CRA to avoid being assessed penalties. (pg. 122)

90. Reduce the sting of infractions by knowing which fines and penalties are tax deductible. (pg. 124)

91. Turn personal loans into business loans and deduct the interest for tax purposes. (pg. 124)

92. Pay down personal loans before business loans to maximize your tax-deductible interest expense. (pg. 124)

93. Structure business loans to turn non-deductible insurance premiums into tax-deductible expenditures. (pg. 125)

94. Deduct your health and dental premiums in your business and save. (pg. 126)

95. Deduct one-half of CPP/QPP contributions and save. (pg. 127)

96. Deduct 100% of meal costs at Remote Work Sites. (pg. 128)

97. Maximize your meal expenses by keeping track of which meals are fully deductible. (pg. 128)

98. Keep detailed records supporting the business nature of trips to camps and lodges to ensure they can be tax deductible. (pg. 130)

99. Itemize cost of meals and beverages at golf courses to ensure deductibility. (pg. 131)

100. Consider non-cash gifts and awards to save your employee's some tax. (pg. 131)

101. Don't exceed the $500 cost limits or give near-cash items or else your employee will be faced with a tax bill on your gift. (pg. 132)

102. Maximize your tax savings on course fees by taking those courses that are fully deductible for income tax purposes. (pg. 132)

103. Review your employer-paid training costs to ensure your staff are not paying too much tax. (pg. 134)

104. Know which conventions are tax deductible and attend accordingly. (pg. 135)

105. When advertising to the Canadian public, advertise with Canadian media to ensure your advertising dollars are tax deductible. (pg. 135)

106. Reduce taxes by not including in your year-end inventory, obsolete or damaged goods. (pg. 136)

107. Provide for doubtful paying customers and defer tax dollars. (pg. 137)

108. If your home is not your principal place of business, designate an area in your home to be used solely for business purposes and conduct client meetings at home. (pg. 140)

109. If your home is your principal place of business, maximize your tax deductions by designating an area in your home to be used exclusively for your business. (pg. 140)

110. Maximize the home area used in your business or minimize the area of your home. (pg. 141)

111. New or increased home costs that are a direct result of your business can be deducted 100% as a business expense. (pg. 142)

112. A separate telephone line for your business is 100% tax deductible. (pg. 142)

113. Keep track of the business portion of home expenses so each year you can deduct them either in the current year or in a profitable year. (pg. 143)

114. Maximize your tax savings by properly classifying the business portion of home expenses from business expenses. (pg. 143)

115. If you have moved your home and your home-based busi-ness, consider claiming moving expenses and save. (pg. 144)

116. Elect not to claim permissible deductions to increase your income so that you won't lose the ability to deduct moving expenses. (pg. 147)

117. Maximize tax savings by knowing the difference between a capital and an expense purchase. (pg. 151)

118. Claim full depreciation on assets not subject to the half-rate rule. (pg. 152)

119. Claim terminal losses to maximize your tax savings. (pg. 153)

120. Delay claiming CCA in times where you may lose the use of the deduction. (pg. 154)

121. When deferring CCA deductions, start by deferring fast-depreciating assets first to provide maximum flexibility. (pg. 154)

122. Purchase assets at the end of the business year instead of the beginning of the next year. (pg. 155)

123. Ensure that your capital purchase is available-for-use by the end of your business year, even if you don't, in fact, use it. (pg. 156)

124. Near your year-end, delay the sale of a capital asset until early the next year. (pg. 156)

125. When purchasing a computer and software at the same time, break out the software portion of the purchase and deduct at the 100% CCA rate. (pg. 157)

126. Elect to include electronic office equipment in a separate CCA class to potentially increase your tax savings on sale. (pg. 158)

127. Elect to include manufacturing and processing machinery and equipment in a separate CCA class to potentially increase your tax savings on sale. (pg. 159)

128. Deduct 100% of the cost of tools costing less than $500. (pg. 159)

129. Deduct CCA on personal assets which are now being used in your business. (pg. 159)

130. Deduct a portion of the cost of assets used both personally and in a business. (pg. 161)

131. Record all business kilometres you drive. (pg. 166)

132. Keep all automotive receipts to support your tax deduction. (pg. 166)

133. If two or more vehicles are used in your business, keep track of the business kilometres on each vehicle to maximize your tax deductions. (pg. 167)

134. Maximize tax savings by using the vehicle with higher operating costs. (pg. 167)

135. Record your odometer readings at the beginning and end of each year. (pg. 167)

136. Schedule client meetings on the way to and from work to increase business kilometres and save taxes. (pg. 168)

137. Maximize your tax savings by purchasing vehicles that are not considered passenger vehicles. (pg. 171)

138. Avoid class 10.1 restrictions by negotiating favourable new vehicle purchase deals. (pg. 173)

139. Maximize your lease deduction by keeping operating expenses out of the lease agreement. (pg. 174)

140. Arrange new car financing so that none of the interest is restricted. (pg. 175)

141. Consider whether to own your personal vehicle personally instead of in a corporation. (pg. 177)

142. When personal kilometres are low, use the 22 cents per personal kilometre method of calculating your operating taxable benefit. (pg. 178)

143. Before purchasing your vehicle, compare the standby charge under the lease option. (pg. 178)

144. Reduce your standby charge by selling your vehicle to one of your other operating companies. (pg. 178)

145. Save time and money: pay yourself a reasonable tax-free car allowance on personally owned vehicles. (pg. 179)

146. Reduce the tax you pay with investment tax credits. (pg. 182)

147. Apply for 40% investment tax credit refund to speed up tax savings. (pg. 183)

148. Apply unused investment tax credits to past and future taxation years. (pg. 183)

149. Reduce CCA claims to use up investment tax credits before they expire. (pg. 183)

150. File your tax return on time to ensure ITC carry backs are accepted by Canada Revenue Agency. (pg. 184)

151. Consider using the Preclaim Project Review Service to save time and money in determining if your project qualifies. (pg. 186)

152. Delay deducting SR&ED expenses to reduce risk of loss carry forwards expiring. (pg. 187)

153. Deduct SR&ED capital expenditures all in one year. (pg. 187)

154. Consider incorporating your business to receive an additional 15% investment tax credit. (pg. 188)

155. Claim your 40% refund of excess investment tax credits on your personal return. (pg. 188)

156. Consider incorporating your business to receive a 100% refund of investment tax credits. (pg. 189)

157. File your SR&ED forms before the deadline or lose the tax benefits forever. (pg. 190)

158. Remember that investment tax credits are included in income when hiring someone to submit your claim. (pg. 191)

159. Determine whether you are eligible to claim an Apprenticeship Job Creation Tax Credit for any new employees. (pg. 191)

160. Review your assessment notice to ensure you're not paying more tax than necessary. (pg. 196)

161. Save time and money by reviewing in detail Canada Revenue Agency's proposed adjustments. (pg. 198)

162. Recommend having Canada Revenue Agency conduct their audit at your accountant's office to minimize disruption and possibly tax. (pg. 199)

163. Complete Form T400A for notice of objections to ensure Canada Revenue Agency processes your objection properly. (pg. 199)

164. File your notice of objection on time to keep your appeal rights alive. (pg. 200)

165. Stop the interest clock by paying disputed tax liabilities. (pg. 201)

166. Request a refund of missed deductions. (pg. 202)

167. Review old tax years for potential tax adjustment before it is too late. (pg. 203)

168. Make a voluntary disclosure and avoid penalty charges. (pg. 203)

169. Save tax and hassles by negotiating the number of years for filing tax returns. (pg. 205)

170. Consider requesting Canada Revenue Agency to reverse interest and penalties. (pg. 206)

Appendix

Statement of Business Income and Loss
For The Period (enter beginning and ending dates)
(The following schedule has been designed to closely resemble Canada Revenue Agency's form T2124, Statement of Business Activities)

	$	$
Income		
Sales income—net of GST/PST and returns, allowances		_____
Reserves deducted last year		_____
Other income		_____
Gross income (total of above three lines) a		_____
Calculation of cost of goods sold		
Opening inventory (include raw materials, goods in process, and finished goods)		_____

Purchases during the year (net of
    returns, allowances, and discounts) ————————
Sub-contracts ————————
Direct wage costs ————————
Other costs ————————
   Total of above five lines ————————
Minus – Closing inventory (include
    raw materials, goods in process,
    and finished goods) ————————
   Cost of goods sold   b ————————
Gross Profit (line a minus line b)   c ————————

	$	$

Business Expenses
Advertising ————————
Bad debts ————————
Business tax, fees, licences, dues,
    memberships, and subscriptions ————————
Delivery, freight and express ————————
Fuel costs (except for motor vehicles) ————————
Insurance (other than for the home) ————————
Interest (other than for the home
    mortgage) ————————
Maintenance and repairs (other than
    for the home or vehicle) ————————
Meals and entertainment (50% only
    —except in Quebec) ————————
Motor vehicle expenses (not including
    capital cost allowance) ————————
Office expenses ————————
Supplies ————————
Legal, accounting, and other
    professional fees ————————
Property taxes (other than for the home) ————————
Rent (other than for the home) ————————

Salaries, wages, and benefits
    (including employer's contributions) ————————

Travel   ————————

Telephone   ————————

Utilities (other than for the home)   ————————

Other expenses   ————————

Capital cost allowance   ————————

Allowance on eligible capital property   ————————

   Total business expenses   d   ————————

Net income (loss) before adjustments
    (line c minus line d)   e   ————————

Adjustments to Net Income (Loss)
For the Period (enter beginning and ending dates)

                                             $

Net income (loss) before adjustments
    (line e from previous page)   f ————————

Your share of line f (include on this
    line your share of the income or loss.
If you are in a partnership, include
    your share of the partnership
    income or loss.)   g ————————

Minus other amounts deductible from
    your share of the net partnership
    income (loss) (attach list)   h ————————

Net income (loss) after adjustments
    (line g minus line h)   i ————————

Minus business-use-of-home expenses
    (from m below)   j ————————

Net income (loss) (line i minus line j)   ————————

Calculation of Business-Use-Of-Home Expenses

Heat   ————————

Electricity   ————————

Insurance   ————————

Mortgage interest   _____
Property taxes   _____
Other expenses   _____
   Subtotal   _____
Minus personal use portion   _____
   Subtotal   _____
Plus amount carried forward from previous year   _____
   Subtotal   k _____
Minus net income (loss) after adjustments from
   line i above (if negative, enter "0")   l _____
Business-use-of-home expenses available for carry
   forward (line k minus line l) if negative, enter "0"   _____
Allowable claim (the lower of amounts on line k or
   on line l) enter this amount on line j above   m _____

Typical Small Business Capital Expenditures
Complete With CCA Class and CCA Rate

Asset Description	CCA Class	CCA Rate
Automobile-passenger vehicle costing < $30,000 or a non-passenger vehicle	10	30%
Automobile-passenger vehicle costing > $30,000	10.1	30%
Automotive equipment	10	30%
Billboards, acquired after 1987[5]	8	20%
Buildings-brick, stone, cement, etc., acquired after 1987	1	4%
Buildings-frame, log, stucco on frame, galvanized iron or corrugated metal if unsupported below ground subject to certain restrictions	6	10%
Calculator	8	20%
Chinaware and cutlery[2]	12	100%
Computer (acquired after March 19, 2007)[1, 3, 4]	50	55%
Computer software[3]	12	100%
Costumes and accessories for earning rental income[2]	12	100%

Cutting part of a machine	12	100%
Dental instruments (costing less than $200)[2]	12	100%
Desk	8	20%
Dies	12	100%
Electrical advertising signs	8	20%
Fax machine[1]	8	20%
Fences	6	10%
Filing cabinet	8	20%
Furniture and equipment not included in any other class	8	20%
Glass tableware[2]	12	100%
Land	N/A	Nil
Linen[2]	12	100%
Machinery and equipment not specifically listed	8	20%

Asset Description	CCA Class	CCA Rate
Machinery and equipment used primarily in manufacturing and processing (acquired after February 25, 1992)	43	30%
Medical equipment (costing less than $200)[2]	12	100%
Metric scales	8	20%
Outdoor advertising billboards acquired after 1987	8	20%
Parking area	17	8%
Photocopier[1]	8	20%
Radio communication equipment	8	20%
Refrigeration equipment	8	20%
Sidewalks	17	8%
Small tools (costing less than $500)[2]	12	100%
Taxicabs	16	40%
Telegraph and telephone equipment	8	20%
Tile drainage—other than for farmers	8	20%
Tractors for hauling freight	16	40%
Trucks, automotive (unless passenger vehicle costing > $24,000)	10	30%
Trucks, for hauling freight	16	40%

Uniforms[2]	12	100%
Video games	8	20%
Video games (coin-operated)	16	40%
Video tapes for lease	12	100%

1 See Round 9 for more details on how to save tax dollars with the purchase of electronic office equipment.

2 The half rate rule does not apply to this asset. The full cost of the asset may be written off in the first year.

3 If purchased to fix year 2000 problem between January 1, 1998 and October 31, 1999, then 100% CCA rate, not subject to the half rate rule.

4 If purchased after March 22, 2004 the CCA rate is 45%. If purchased before March 22, 2004 the CCA rate is 30%.

5. Under proposed legislation, the rate for non-residential buildings acquired after March 18, 2007, used for manufacturing and processing in Canada of goods for sale or lease is 10%. For all other non-residential buildings, the rate will increase to 6%. In order to be eligible for these increased rates, the building must be placed into a separate class.

Index